A Concise Introduction to MS-DOS

ALSO AVAILABLE

A Concise Introduction to MS-DOS

by

Noel Kantaris

BERNARD BABANI (publishing) LTD.
THE GRAMPIANS
SHEPHERDS BUSH ROAD
LONDON W6 7NF
ENGLAND

PLEASE NOTE

Although every care has been taken with the production of this book to ensure that any projects, designs, modifications and/or programs, etc., contained herewith, operate in a correct and safe manner and also that any components specified are normally available in Great Britain, the Publishers and Author(s) do not accept responsibility in any way for the failure (including fault in design) of any project, design, modification or program to work correctly or to cause damage to any equipment that it may be connected to or used in conjunction with, or in respect of any other damage or injury that may be so caused, nor do the Publishers accept responsibility in any way for the failure to obtain specified components.

Notice is also given that if equipment that is still under warranty is modified in any way or used or connected with home-built equipment then that warranty may be void.

First Published - August 1987
Revised Edition - January 1989
Reprinted - 1989, 1990, 1991
Revised Edition - January 1992
Reprinted - 1993
Revised Edition - January 1995

British Library Cataloguing in Publication Data:

Kantaris, Noel
    A concise introduction to MS-DOS
    1. MS-DOS (Computer operating system)
    I. Title
    005.4'3 qa76.6

ISBN 0 85934 177 1

Printed and Bound in Great Britain by Cox & Wyman Ltd, Reading

ABOUT THIS BOOK

To help the beginner, this concise guide to MS/PC-DOS, has been written with an underlying structure based on 'what you need to know first, appears first'. However, the book is also circular, which means that you don't have to start at the beginning and go to the end. The more experienced user can start from any section, as each section has been designed to be self contained.

This book does not seek to replace the documentation you receive with your operating system, but only to supplement and explain it. No previous knowledge of the operating system is assumed, but the book does not describe how to set up your computer hardware, optimise system resources through memory management and disc compression, or how to install and run Microsoft Windows. If you need to know more about these advanced topics, then may we suggest that you also refer to either *MS-DOS 6 Explained* (BP341) or *A Concise User's Guide to MS-DOS 5* (BP318), depending on your system's version of DOS, and/or *A Concise User's Guide to Windows 3.1* (BP325). These books are also published by BERNARD BABANI (publishing) Ltd.

This book covers all the latest DOS versions, including the whole range of versions 3.x, 4.x, 5.0, and 6.x as implemented by Microsoft and IBM for the IBM *compatible* personal micro-computer. A separate section of the book deals with the enhancements to be found in these versions, including MSBackup for backing up you data (MS-DOS 6.x versions only), Edit, the full screen editor (available with DOS versions 5.0 & 6.x), DOS Shell, the menu-driven graphical interface (available with versions 4.x & 5.0), and Edlin, the line editor of pre-DOS 5.0 versions.

This book was written with the busy person in mind. You don't need to read hundreds of pages of information to find out most there is to know about the subject, when fewer pages on selected topics can do the same thing quite adequately! In particular, the book seeks to bring to the forefront and exploit the inherent simplicity in the DOS operating system by presenting, with examples, the principles of what you need to know, when you need to know them.

At the same time, the book has been written in such a way as to also act as a reference guide, long after you have mastered most DOS commands. To this end, a summary of the commands supported by the MS-DOS operating system is given in the penultimate chapter of this book. The commands are explained with relevant examples and, as such, the section can serve as a quick reference guide to the Disc Operating System. The last chapter of the book is devoted to a 'Glossary of Terms' which can enhance the understanding of those who are new to the world of microcomputers.

With the help of this book, it is hoped that you will be able to get the most out of your computer in terms of efficiency, productivity and enjoyment, and that you will be able to do it in the shortest, most effective and informative way.

If you would like to purchase a floppy disc containing all the files/programs which appear in this, or any other listed book(s) by the same author(s), then fill-in the form at the back of the book and send it to P. R. M. Oliver at the stipulated address.

ACKNOWLEDGEMENTS

I would like to thank colleagues at the Camborne School of Mines for the helpful tips and suggestions which assisted me in the writing of this book.

ABOUT THE AUTHOR

Graduated in Electrical Engineering at Bristol University and
after spending three years in the Electronics Industry in
London, took up a Tutorship in Physics at the University of
Queensland. Research interests in Ionospheric Physics, led
to the degrees of M.E. in Electronics and Ph.D. in Physics.
On return to the UK, he took up a Post-Doctoral Research
Fellowship in Radio Physics at the University of Leicester,
and then in 1973 a lecturing position in Engineering at the
Camborne School of Mines, Cornwall, (part of Exeter
University), where since 1978 he has also assumed the
responsibility for the Computing Department.

TRADEMARKS

CONTENTS

1. INTRODUCTION

Most 16-bit microcomputers use Microsoft's Disc Operating System (MS-DOS) as the prime means of interaction between user and computer. Owners of IBM PCs know this operating system as PC-DOS or DOS, which is IBM's implementation of MS-DOS. The name MS-DOS will be used throughout this book to distinguish this operating system from another popular one, namely Digital Research's DR-DOS, now owned by Novell.

Versions of MS-DOS

Since its inception in 1981, MS-DOS has been the standard operating system for personal computers and by now is being used by more than 50 million people. As the number of users increased over the years, so too has the complexity of applications run on their PCs. To meet these ever increasing demands, MS-DOS has also increased its functionality several times in the form of *new* versions, as shown in the table below.

Version	Date	Main changes in functionality
1.0	1981	Original Disc Operating System 86-QDOS renamed MS-DOS.
1.25	1982	Support for double-sided discs. IBM calls this PC-DOS 1.1.
2.0	1983	Support for a 10MB hard disc, subdirectories, and 360KB floppy discs.
2.11	1983	Support for extended character set.
3.0	1984	Support for 1.2MB floppy disc and larger capacity hard disc (up to 32MB).
3.1	1984	Support for PC networks.
3.2	1986	Support for 3½" floppy disc.
3.3	1987	Support for PS/2 computer range, 1.44MB, 3½" floppy discs, partitioning of hard discs, and additional codepages.

4.0	1988	Support for extended memory (EMS), hard disc partitions beyond 32MB (up to 2GB), and the graphical user interface DOS shell.
4.01	1989	Fix bugs in 4.0 version.
5.0	1991	Support for the 2.88MB floppy disc, running DOS in high memory and certain device drivers in upper memory. Adopts a full screen editor and context sensitive help.
6.0	1993	Support for Double Space, Anti-Virus, and Defragmenter disc utilities. Adds the Move and Deltree commands and a new MSBACKUP utility. Provides for multiple start-up configurations.
6.2	1993	Support for a one-pass DISK-COPY, CD-ROM caching and SCANDISK which replaces the CHKDSK command. Includes DoubleGuard to protect memory used by Double Space, which can now be uninstalled.

MS-DOS versions 4.x and 5.0, differed in one major aspect from earlier versions of MS-DOS. This was due to the inclusion of the DOS Shell utility - a menu-driven graphical interface - which was introduced in an attempt to make DOS easier to use. Although Microsoft has stopped distributing the DOS Shell utility with version 6.2, it has not withdrawn support for it, therefore its use is explained in Appendix A.

What You Need to Know
It is assumed here that the reader is familiar with handling floppy discs, floppy and hard disc drives, and that the installation manual which comes with every microcomputer has been read and complied with.

What this book tries to do is supplement the MS-DOS operating manual by explaining the various commands with ample working examples which is something that user manuals seldom seem to do; they are excellent for reference purposes, for those who already know, but learning from them is almost impossible.

The MS-DOS operating system consists of a collection of small, specialised programs that make up the working environment which allows you to create and save programs, copy or delete data files from disc or perform other input and output (I/O) operations, such as finding a program or a file on a particular disc or printing the contents of that file on the printer. In general, MS-DOS is the micro's administrator and understanding the way it works is very important. Running a computer without understanding its operating system is similar to trying to run a library without any knowledge of librarianship. Very soon chaos will be the order of the day.

At first sight, the various commands within MS-DOS might appear difficult to understand and remember, particularly if the first encounter with them is made through the operating manual which was designed, after all, to act as a reference manual and was never intended to be used to learn from. However, there is a certain simplicity in the way MS-DOS likes to receive instructions and once this simplicity is understood, using its various commands becomes natural.

This book seeks to bring to the forefront, and exploit, this inherent simplicity in MS-DOS commands by presenting, with examples, the principles of what you need to know, when you need to know them. However, in the last chapter of the book, you will find a summary of *all* the MS-DOS commands, explained with appropriate and relevant examples, which will serve as a quick reference guide long after you have mastered most of the MS-DOS commands.

Furthermore, to help the newcomer to DOS, a glossary of terms is included in the last chapter of the book.

The Structure of MS-DOS
To learn to use MS-DOS you must understand its underlying structure. The various MS-DOS administrative functions are contained in three, separate, main files (later on, we will explain what files mean and their naming convention).

These are:

    MSDOS.SYS
    IO.SYS
    COMMAND.COM

or IBMDOS.COM, IBMBIO.COM and COMMAND.COM, in the case of the IBM PC.

The first file is the core of the operating system, while the second one, also called the Basic Input Output System (BIOS), allows the core to communicate with the hardware. It is the BIOS that is adapted by manufacturers of different hardware so that the operating system can appear to function in the same way, even though there might be differences in hardware design. The last file, COMMAND.COM, is the Command Processor which analyses what is typed at the keyboard, and if correct, finds and starts execution of the appropriate command.

MS-DOS has between thirty and forty built-in commands (depending on version), normally referred to as 'internal commands', instantly available to the user as they reside in memory. In addition to these internal commands, there are between sixty and ninety 'external' commands which are to be found on the MS-DOS distribution discs. The machine program which makes up each of these external commands is saved in a *file* under an appropriate name with a .COM or .EXE extension to the filename (more about this later). Collectively, these internal and external commands make up the computer's Disc Operating System (DOS). These commands will be examined in detail in the following chapters of this book.

Booting up the System:

Whenever you start your computer by switching on the power, the system is booted up, which is normally indicated by the appearance of a C> or A> prompt, for booting from a hard or floppy disc drive, respectively. However, if you are running the DOS Shell (or some other interface), you might not see the usual C> prompt.

To boot the system, the MS-DOS System files must have been transferred on the C: drive, for a hard disc-based system, or a disc which contains the System files (known as the System disc), must be in the A: drive, for a floppy disc-based system. It is assumed here that you have followed the manufacturer's instructions on how to format the hard disc and transfer the System and all other files from the distribution discs onto it. This procedure is rarely required these days, as most computers are sold with pre-formatted hard discs and pre-loaded with MS-DOS. If this is not the case, then do so before going on any further.

After successfully booting up the system, display a listing of the directory by typing **DIR** at the prompt and pressing <Enter>. This will reveal the contents of your disc, but neither of the first two System files (MSDOS.SYS and IO.SYS) will appear on the directory list as they are hidden. Only the third file (COMMAND.COM) will be displayed.

In addition to these three special files, there are a number of other files which perform various important tasks. These files are collectively known as the DOS utilities and will be examined in detail later. To be able to distinguish between disc drives, MS-DOS refers to them by a letter followed by a colon, i.e. C: or A: for the prime drive of the appropriate system. In a twin floppy disc-based system, there are two drives; A: and B:, with drive A: being the leftmost or uppermost of the two, while on a hard disc-based system there is a hard disc drive, C: (additional ones are named D:, E:, and so on) and a floppy disc drive A: (with one possible extra, named B:). DOS allows you to also refer to drive A: as drive B:, so that you can copy files from one floppy disc to another using a single floppy disc drive. Users on networked systems can access a network hard disc by assigning it as another drive on their micro, namely as E: or Z:

On booting up the micro from a MS-DOS System disc, the following tasks are performed:

- A self test on its Random Access Memory (RAM) is performed.

- A check is made to see if a floppy disc is in drive A:, and if there is, whether it is a System disc. If it is, it boots the system from the A: drive.

- If no floppy exists in drive A:, an attempt is made to boot the system from drive C:, if there is one, otherwise in the case of the IBM, it goes into Read Only Memory (ROM) based BASIC.

- Configures the system by executing the CONFIG.SYS file.

- Reads the BIOS and the MS-DOS operating system.

- Loads into RAM the COMMAND.COM file so that internal commands can be made available instantly.

- Executes the commands within the AUTOEXEC.BAT file, if one exists, otherwise it asks for the Date and Time which can be reset at this point. Pressing the <Enter> key, confirms what is displayed.

Should you receive any error message while these tasks are being performed, you could restart the process, after rectifying the error, by pressing simultaneously the three keys marked **Ctrl**, **Alt** and **Del**, shown as <Ctrl+Alt+Del> in the rest of the book. This will re-boot the system and is referred to as a 'warm re-boot'. In contrast, re-booting the system by either switching the power off and then back on again or pressing the 'Reset' button, is referred to as a 'cold re-boot'.

Internal DOS Commands

MS-DOS has between thirty and forty internal commands (depending on version) built into it which are instantly available as they reside in memory. These are listed below.

Command	*Meaning*
BREAK	Sets the Ctrl+Break check on or off. Used either at the command prompt or in the CONFIG.SYS file.
BUFFERS	Allocates memory for a specified number of disc buffers from within your CONFIG.SYS file.
CALL	Calls one batch file from another without exiting from the first one.
CD or CHDIR	Changes the current directory.

CHCP	Displays or changes the active code page.
CLS	Clears the screen.
COPY	Copies files.
CTTY	Changes the standard Input/Output device.
DATE	Displays or sets the system date.
DEL	Deletes the specified files.
DEVICE	Loads a specified device driver into memory from within your CONFIG.SYS file.
DIR	Displays the disc directory.
DOS	Specifies from within your CONFIG.SYS file that DOS should maintain a link to the upper memory area, load part of itself into high memory area (HMA), or both.
ECHO	Sets Echo to on or off.
ERASE	See DEL command.
EXIT	Exits to the previous command level.
FCBS	Specifies from within your CONFIG.SYS file the number of File Control Blocks (FCBs) that DOS can have open at the same time.
FILES	Specifies from within your CONFIG.SYS file the number of files that DOS can access at one time.
FOR	Repeats a command for each item in a set.
GOTO	Jumps to a labelled line within the same batch file.
IF	Allows conditional execution of commands within a batch file.
INCLUDE	Includes from within your CONFIG.SYS file the contents of one configuration block within another.
INSTALL	Loads from within your CONFIG.SYS file a memory-resident program into memory.

LASTDRIVE	Specifies from within your CONFIG.SYS file the maximum number of drives you can access.
LH (LOADHIGH)	Loads a program into upper memory.
MD or MKDIR	Makes (creates) a new directory.
NUMLOCK	Specifies from within your CONFIG.SYS file whether the NUMLOCK key is set ON or OFF.
PATH	Searches alternative directories.
PAUSE	Pauses execution of the batch file.
PROMPT	Changes the system prompt.
RD or RMDIR	Removes (deletes) a directory.
REM	Allows remarks to be added in a batch file.
REN or RENAME	Renames files.
SET	Changes the system parameters.
SHELL	Specifies from within CONFIG.SYS the location of the command interpreter you want DOS to use.
SHIFT	Allows more than 10 replaceable parameters in a batch file.
STACKS	Supports the dynamic use of data stacks to handle hardware interrupts. This command can only be used from within your CONFIG.SYS file.
SUBMENU	Defines from within CONFIG.SYS an item on a start-up menu that, when selected, displays another set of options.
SWITCHES	Specifies from within CONFIG.SYS special DOS options.
TIME	Displays or sets the system time.
TYPE	Displays a specified text file.
VER	Displays the MS-DOS version.
VERIFY	Checks disc writing.
VOL	Displays the disc volume label.

The internal DOS commands (most of which will be explained later), together with the rest of the operating system, occupy between 40 and 65KB of RAM (depending on version), as they are loaded into memory on booting up the system.

Where exactly in memory these commands are loaded, depends on the version of DOS being used and the type of processor in your system.

For example, if you were using an MS-DOS version prior to version 5, then all the DOS commands would load in 'conventional' memory, which is the first 640KB of memory in your computer. If you are using MS-DOS version 5 or 6, in a computer with Intel's 80286 or higher processor, part of the DOS commands could be loaded into 'extended' memory (the memory between 1 and 16MB - or even higher on 80386 and 80486 machines), freeing at least 45KB of 'conventional' memory for your DOS applications.

Illustrating Internal DOS Commands

As an illustration of internal DOS commands, consider the two which allow you to re-set the date and time of your computer's internal clock.

DOS Shell Users: In order to emulate what is presented below, it will be necessary to select the 'Command Prompt' option from the Main menu at the lower half of the DOS Shell screen.

The DATE & TIME Commands:

Your computer is equipped with an internal clock, whose date and time can be changed. Typing the command

```
DATE
```

at the C> prompt, evokes the response

```
Current date is dd/mm/yy
Enter new date:
```

at which point you can either type a new date or press <Enter> to indicate no change. The above date format assumes that you have included the command COUNTRY=xxx (or equivalent in the case of PC-DOS 3.3), where xxx is a three digit code representing your country, in your CONFIG.SYS file (to be discussed later), otherwise the date will be shown in mm/dd/yy format.

Similarly, typing the command

```
TIME
```

at the prompt, evokes the response

```
Current time is Hrs:Mins:Secs
Enter new time:
```

at which point you can either type a new time or press <Enter> to indicate that time is not to be changed.

External DOS Commands
DOS provides between sixty and ninety additional commands which, to avoid eating up more of the computer's memory, reside on disc. These are known as external commands and can only be invoked if a disc containing the required files is accessible. In the case of a floppy disc-based system some of these files will be found on the System disc in the A: drive (DOS can be installed on a floppy disc). For a hard disc-based system, these additional commands would have been transferred onto the DOS subdirectory of the C: drive (shown as \DOS - more about subdirectories later) and can be accessed directly from it.

Files and the Disc Directory
To see a list of the DOS directory, type **DIR \DOS** at the C> prompt (for a hard disc-based system) or type **DIR** at the A> prompt (for a floppy disc-based system), and press <Enter>.

DOS Shell Users: Select the DOS subdirectory (by pointing and clicking with the mouse, or pressing the <Tab> key to move to the 'Directory Tree' and using the directional keys to highlight the option). If you want to type the **DIR \DOS** command, select the 'Command Prompt' option from the 'Main' menu of the DOS Shell.

Amongst the many files to be listed will be the ones shown on the facing page, the name, size and creation dates of which depend on the version of MS-DOS you are running on your computer - the ones shown here are the ones included with MS-DOS 6.2.

10

Filename	Extension	Size	Date	Time
APPEND	EXE	10774	30/09/93	6:20
CHKDSK	EXE	12241	30/09/93	6:20
COMMAND	COM	54619	30/09/93	6:20
DISKCOPY	COM	13335	30/09/93	6:20
FORMAT	COM	22916	30/09/93	6:20
KEYBOARD	SYS	34598	30/09/93	6:20
LABEL	EXE	9390	10/03/93	6:00
OS2	TXT	6358	10/03/93	6:00
PRINT	EXE	15656	30/09/93	6:20
QBASIC	HLP	130881	10/03/93	6:00
RESTORE	EXE	38342	30/09/93	6:20
SCANDISK	EXE	119761	30/09/93	6:20
SORT	EXE	6938	30/09/93	6:20
XCOPY	EXE	16930	30/09/93	6:20

Note that a filename consists of up to 8 alphanumeric characters (letters and numbers only) and has a three letter extension, separated from the filename by a period, i.e., COMMAND.COM or CONFIG.SYS, without any spaces in between, unlike the listing appearing on your screen, where the periods have been omitted and the extensions have been tabulated as above.

Some of these files might have different extensions from the ones shown above, i.e., .EXE might appear as .COM in your system, as the extensions tend to differ for different versions of MS-DOS. The size of each file (in bytes) is also given on the listing together with the date and time it was created, which again might differ for different versions.

The extensions .COM, .SYS and .EXE (which stand for 'Command', 'System' and 'Executable') are the most common extensions of the files which make up MS-DOS. They contain instructions which are executed directly by the computer. Other extensions commonly used by programs or users are:

```
.BAK .BAS .BAT .DAT .DOC .HLP .TXT .TMP
```

which indicate 'back-up' files, 'Basic' programs, 'batch' files, 'data' files, 'document' files, 'help' files, 'text' files and 'temporary' files, respectively.

The DIR Switches:

Returning to the result of issuing the DIR command; what is more likely to have happened in your case is that the listing of the first half of the files on your disc will have scrolled out of view. In all, there could be up to ninety utility files on the DOS subdirectory and you can only see the last twenty or so.

To stop the scrolling of a long directory, use the /P switch after the DIR command, as follows:

```
DIR \DOS /P
```

which will page the directory, displaying twenty files at a time. Alternatively, you could see all these files on your screen by using the /W switch, as follows:

```
DIR \DOS /W
```

which lists the files in 'wide' format, as follows:

APPEND	EXE	CHKDSK	EXE	COMMAND	COM
DISKCOPY	COM	FORMAT	COM	KEYBOARD	SYS
LABEL	EXE	OS2	TXT	PRINT	EXE
QBASIC	HLP	RESTORE	EXE	SCANDISK	EXE
SORT	EXE	XCOPY	EXE		

Note that in this case the information relating to the size of each file and the date and time of its creation has been omitted from the listing.

Using Wildcard Characters:

You can limit the information which appears on your screen by being more selective with the use of wildcards. For example, to list all the .EXE files on your disc, type

```
DIR \DOS\*.EXE
```

where the wildcard character '*' stands for 'all' files.

Note that spaces are very important to MS-DOS. Had you not included a space after DIR in the above command, MS-DOS would have responded with its favoured error message,

12

which does not tell you very much, except that MS-DOS does not understand you!

The wildcard character '*' can also be used as part of the filename. For example,

```
DIR \DOS\DOS*.*
```

will list all the files with all extensions on the logged drive, starting with the three characters DOS, irrespective of the ending of the filenames. There are 9 such files in MS-DOS 5 and 6.

The full MS-DOS command should also specify which drive you want to access, but can be omitted if the command refers to the currently logged drive. Thus,

```
DIR A:DOS*.*
```
will access the specified files on drive A:, while

```
DIR B:DOS*.*
```
will access the specified files on drive B:.

Alternatively, you can change the logged drive by simply typing its identification letter at the prompt. For example,

```
C>A:
```
will change the logged drive, indicated by changing the prompt, to

```
A>_
```

which indicates that the currently logged drive is now A:. All further commands which do not specify a different drive, will access drive A:. To revert back to the previously logged drive, type C: at the A> prompt.

A more precise wildcard is the query character '?' which can be substituted for a single character in a filename. For example, assuming that there are several consecutively numbered files on your disc with filenames TEXT1.DOC to TEXT999.DOC, typing

```
DIR TEXT?.DOC
```

will list all files with the extension .DOC, from TEXT1 to TEXT9, but not those within the range TEXT10 to TEXT999. On the other hand, using two consecutive query characters in the filename, such as

```
DIR TEXT??.DOC
```

will list all files with the extension .DOC, from TEXT1 to TEXT99, but exclude those within the range TEXT100 to TEXT999.

To list all the files from TEXT1 to TEXT999 you must use the wildcard character '*' in place of the single query, as follows:

```
DIR TEXT*.DOC
```

Finally, typing

```
DIR *.*
```

will display all files with all extensions which, of course, has the same effect as typing

```
DIR
```

Nevertheless, the *.* is worth noting as it is the most useful three-character combination in MS-DOS and will be mainly used in housekeeping commands to be explained later.

Should you ever want to find out whether a particular file exists on a disc, just type its name after the DIR command, but specifying the subdirectory in which the file is to be found. If the file exists, MS-DOS will display it, otherwise the message

```
File not found
```

will appear on your screen.

Rules for Entering Commands

Commands can be entered in either uppercase or lower-case letters, but you must provide a space between the command and its parameters. For example, to obtain a listing of all the .EXE files on the floppy in the A: drive in wide format, you can either type

```
DIR A:*.EXE /W
```

or

```
dir a:*.exe /w
```

but you must type one space between the R (or r) and the drive identification name. The space between the E (or e) and the slash sign (/) is optional; its presence only serves to improve readability.

If DOS informs you that you have made a mistake while typing a command - you will soon know this because on pressing the <Enter> key, DOS will reply with

```
Bad command or file name
```

you can edit what you have typed previously by pressing the right arrow key which causes DOS to display the command a letter at a time. Keep pressing the right arrow key until you have reached the offending part of the command which can be over-typed. If need be, you can add extra letters to the command by pressing the <Ins> key, or remove extra letters by pressing the <Del> key, then you can use the right arrow key again to continue revealing the rest of the command one letter at a time, or press the **F3** function key to reveal the rest of the command.

Upgrading to DOS Version 6.2

Generally it is worth upgrading from an earlier version of MS-DOS to the current version, because of the inclusion of new and improved commands and utility programs that can add to the efficiency of your computer. For example, MS-DOS 6.2 includes the following new or improved features:

- A utility which compresses files before storing them on either your hard or floppy discs.

- A utility that optimises your computer's memory by moving device drivers and memory-resident programs into upper memory, thus freeing conventional memory so that programs can run faster and more efficiently.

- A utility that identifies and removes more than one thousand known viruses from your computer system.

- A Backup utility that makes backing up your data very easy indeed.

- An undelete utility that allows you to select one of three levels of protection in case you accidentally delete a file.

- The ability to define more than one configuration for your system in your CONFIG.SYS file.

- A utility that defragments (reorganises) files on your hard disc so they are contiguous, which minimises access time of these files.

- An Interlnk utility that allows easy transfer of files between computers.

In this book, only the Backup utility will be discussed. If you are running MS-DOS 6.x and you want to know more about the above utilities, then may we suggest that you refer to the higher level book *MS-DOS 6 Explained* (BP341) also published by BERNARD BABANI (publishing) Ltd.

2. MANAGING DISC FILES

MS-DOS provides several commands which help you to manage your disc files efficiently. Some of these commands are internal and some are external. If the commands under discussion are external commands and your computer is a twin-floppy system, it will be pointed out so you can insert the System disc in the logged drive which is the drive indicated by letter on the screen prompt.

The FORMAT Command

One of the first things you will need to do, as a new user, is to make a working copy of your System disc, or favoured software package, or just a back-up copy of your programs or data. Such packages and/or data are far too valuable in terms of money or time invested in producing them to be used continually without the safeguard of back-up copies.

Again, it is assumed that in the case of a hard disc-based system, your hard disc has already been formatted according to your manufacturer's instructions when setting up the system, and that all the MS-DOS external command files have been transferred onto it.

A new floppy disc must be formatted before it can be used by your computer's operating system. A floppy disc that has been formatted in one computer, can only be used in another computer if they are compatible and use the same operating system.

To format a disc, in the case of a hard disc-based system where the logged drive will be drive C:, insert the new floppy disc in the A: drive and type.

```
C>FORMAT A:/S/V
```

In the case of a twin-floppy system, insert the System disc in the A: drive, as FORMAT is an external command and needs to be loaded into RAM from the System disc, then insert the new floppy disc in the B: drive and type

```
A>FORMAT B:/S/V
```

Drive C: (or A: in the case of a floppy disc) is accessed momentarily, the FORMAT utility file is loaded into RAM and executed. You are then given instructions to insert a floppy disc in drive A: (or B: in the case of a twin-floppy disc system), and press <Enter> to begin. Be very careful never to format an already formatted disc (particularly the C: drive), as *all* files that might be on it will be lost.

The two switches, typed after the slash character (/), have the following meaning:

The /S switch instructs MS-DOS to copy the hidden system files and the COMMAND.COM file onto the newly formatted disc. This will be required if you intend to use the disc to boot up the system, but not otherwise.

The /V switch allows you to give a volume label to your new disc, after formatting is completed.

DOS Shell Users: To format a floppy disc select the **Disk Utilities** option from the 'Main' group of programs, then use the **Format** command and follow the instructions given on the screen.

Type and Size of Discs:

There are some additional switches that can be used with the FORMAT command (whether you are using the DOS Shell or not) which, however, are dependent on the type of disc drive being used and size of disc. These are as follows:

Disc type	Disc size	Switches
160/180KB	5 ¼ "	/f:size, /b, /s, /u, /q, /1, /8, /4
320/360KB	5 ¼ "	/f:size, /b, /s, /u, /q, /1, /8, /4
1.2MB	5 ¼ "	/f:size, /b, /s, /u, /q, /4, /t, /n
720KB/1.44MB	3 ½ "	/f:size, /b, /s, /u, /q, /t, /n
2.88MB	3 ½ "	/f:size, /b, /s, /u, /q.

where

/f:*size* specifies the size of the floppy disc to format. This switch can be used instead of the /t and /n switches. Use one of the following values for size, which specifies the capacity of the disc in Kbytes:

160/180; single-sided, double-density 5¼" discs,
320/360; double-sided, double-density 5¼" discs,
720; double-sided, double-density 3½" discs,
1200; double-sided, high-density 5¼" discs,
1440; double-sided, high-density 3½" discs,
2880; 2.88MB, double-sided, 3½" discs.

/b   reserves space for the system files IO.SYS and MSDOS.SYS on a newly formatted disc

/s   copies the operating system files IO.SYS, MSDOS.SYS, and COMMAND.COM from the system's start-up drive to the newly formatted disc

/u   specifies an unconditional format operation for a disc, which destroys all existing data on the disc and prevents you from later unformatting the disc

/q   deletes the file allocation table (FAT) and the root directory of a previously formatted disc, but does not scan the disc for bad sectors

/1   formats only one side of the disc (seldom used)

/8   formats 8 sectors per track (seldom used)

/4   formats 40 tracks with 9 sectors per track for 360 Kbytes using a 1.2 Mbyte high-capacity disc drive. This switch must be used if you are using double-density, but not high-capacity discs in a 1.2 Mbyte drive

/t   specifies the number of tracks, written as /t:40 for forty tracks. To format a 720 Kbytes double-sided disc in a high-capacity 3.5" disc drive (1.44 Mbytes), use switches t:80/n:9

/n   specifies the number of sectors per track to format, written as /n:9 for nine sectors.

Switches f:*size*, /b, /u, and /q, are new to MS-DOS 5 and 6.x, while switches /1, /4, and /8 are kept for backward compatibility to earlier versions of DOS. If switches /t or /n are specified, then both parameters must be entered. All other switches can be used separately or omitted altogether from the command. Omitting the /s switch saves disc space.

19

The SYS Command

Should you change your mind after you have formatted a disc without the use of the /s switch, you can use the external SYS command to transfer the System files from the system start-up drive onto a previously formatted disc, inserted in another drive. The command takes the form:

C>SYS A: in the case of a hard disc-based system, or

A>SYS B: in the case of a floppy disc-based system.

To successfully transfer the operating system to a disc with this method, the disc must either be newly formatted or else have space on it for the transfer of the operating system, by perhaps already having a different version of it on the target disc, or by having used the /u switch.

Finally, note that the SYS command transfers only the hidden files of the operating system and the COMMAND.COM file, which means that you must use the COPY command (see next section) to transfer the CONFIG.SYS and AUTOEXEC.BAT files.

Differences Between Disc Drives:

The PC, XT and compatibles have 360 Kbyte double-sided, double-density disc drives. Discs are formatted with 40 tracks per side, 9 sectors per track with 0.5 Kbyte of information per sector, resulting in 360 Kbyte capacity.

The IBM AT, XT286 and compatibles have 1.2 Mbytes high-capacity double-sided disc drives. Discs are formatted with 80 tracks per side, 15 sectors per track with 0.5 Kbyte of information per sector resulting in 1.2 Mbytes capacity. However, each track takes the same physical space as that of the 360 Kbyte drive, the difference being that the tracks that are half the width of the 360 Kbyte drive.

Discs formatted on 1.2 Mbyte disc drives with the /4 option use only one half of the width of each of the 40 tracks. This information can easily be read by a 360 Kbyte drive (as a result of tolerance in signal level), provided the other half of the track is completely clear. Should you now use the 360 Kbyte drive to write to the disc, information is written to the full width of the track which can still be read by the 1.2 Mbyte disc drive (again, as a result of tolerance in signal level).

However, any subsequent writing to such a disc using the 1.2 Mbyte drive, results in changes to only one half of the track width. The result is half a track containing the new information with the corresponding other half of the same track containing the old, half-overwritten information, which makes it impossible for the 360 Kbyte disc drive to make any sense of it. Thus, to avoid such incompatibilities between disc drives, always format double-density discs in a 360 Kbyte drive. Attempting to format a double-density disc to 1.2 Mbytes will result in many bad sectors with future loss of data becoming highly possible.

There are no such problems arising from the use of 3.5" discs which have been formatted as 720 Kbytes in a high-capacity (1.44 Mbytes) disc drive and subsequently used to read or write to them by either a 720 Kbyte or a 1.44 Mbyte disc drive. Again, avoid formatting non high-density discs to 1.44 Mbytes. If, on the other hand, you format accidentally a high-density disc to 720 Kbytes, (this can happen if you use the DISKCOPY command with pre-DOS 5 versions to copy files from a 720 Kbytes disc to a high-capacity unformatted disc), do not attempt to re-format the high-capacity disc to 1.44 Mbytes, because the higher current used by the disc drive to format it to 720 Kbytes can not be wiped out by the reformatting process.

The COPY Command

To copy all files on the disc in the logged drive to the disc in the A: drive, type

```
C>COPY *.* A:
```

Note the most useful three-character combination in MS-DOS, namely *.* which means 'all filenames with all extensions'.

However, if you wanted to copy a set of files from drive A: to drive C:, while being logged onto the C: drive, type

```
C>COPY A:*.DOC C:
```

which means 'copy from the A: drive all the files with extension .DOC to the C: drive'.

21

The /v switch can be used at the end of the COPY command to force MS-DOS to verify that the file(s) it has copied can be read. For example,

```
C>COPY \DOS\FORMAT.COM A:/V
```

will copy the formatting utility file FORMAT.COM from the \DOS directory of the logged drive to the A: drive and force verification that the file can be read.

DOS Shell Users: First select the file(s) you want to copy, then use the **File, Copy** command.

The DISKCOPY Command

Both the formatting and copying can be done in one go by using the DISKCOPY command, as follows:

```
C>DISKCOPY A: B:
```

which will copy all the files and subdirectories from the A: drive, to the B: drive and format the disk in the B: drive at the same time, if not already formatted.

However, if the disc in the B: drive is already formatted, but at different capacity to that in the A: drive, and you are using a version of DOS prior to version 5, then the disc in the B: drive is reformatted to the same capacity as that in the A: drive. This problem has been overcome with MS-DOS version 5 and 6.

DOS Shell Users: Select the **Disk Copy** program in the Disk Utilities.

You can not use the DISKCOPY command to copy files from a floppy disc to a hard disc, or to copy files between two floppy discs of different size (such as 3½" and 5¼" discs).

Note: Sometimes it is preferable to use the FORMAT and COPY commands rather than the DISKCOPY command when copying all files from one disc to another. The reason is that bad sectors are frozen out when formatting a disc and the subsequent use of COPY, avoids these sectors. The DISKCOPY command on the other hand, seeks to make an identical copy (sector by sector) of the original disc which means that it attempts to write on bad sectors, if any, which might lead to an unsuccessful copy operation.

The DISKCOMP Command

This external utility is mostly needed if you use the DISKCOPY command. The command compares the contents of two discs, and takes the following form:

`C>DISKCOMP A: B:`   compares the discs in the A: and the B: drives. For single-floppy drive systems use A: A:, in which case you will be prompted to insert each disc, as required.

The DELETE & UNDELETE Commands

Unwanted files on a disc can be deleted, as follows:

`C>DEL EXAMPLE.TMP`   deletes EXAMPLE.TMP on the C: drive

`C>DEL A:EXAMPLE.TMP`   deletes EXAMPLE.TMP on the A: drive

`A>DEL *.*`   deletes all files on the logged drive.

Luckily, the use of the DEL *.* command evokes the response

`Are you sure? (Y/N)`

which acts as a safety net. It is a good idea to always check what you are about to delete from your disc by first using the DIR command.

For example, say you intend to delete all the .TMP files from your disc. First use DIR *.TMP and if what is displayed on screen is what you want to delete, then type DEL and press the **F3** function key. This has the effect of displaying on the screen the last command you typed on the keyboard, minus the characters you typed prior to pressing the **F3** key. Thus, DEL replaces DIR and the use of **F3** displays the rest of the command. In this way you avoid making any mistakes by re-typing.

As you will, no doubt, use this command at some time or another on your C: drive, it would be prudent to copy both your AUTOEXEC.BAT and CONFIG.SYS files into your DOS directory (see next chapter). In this way you will have copies of these vital files away from harm's reach!

DOS Shell Users: First select the file(s) you want to delete, and then use the **File, Delete** command.

With MS-DOS 5 and 6, you can use the UNDELETE command to recover deleted files. To test this command, first make a copy of your AUTOEXEC.BAT file by typing:

```
C>COPY AUTOEXEC.BAT TEST
```

DOS Shell Users: Use the **File, Copy** command. Then, use the **Delete** command to delete the file TEST.

To undelete a deleted file, type the command

```
C>UNDELETE TEST
```

at the C> prompt. This causes DOS to display a screen in which it asks you to supply the first letter of the name of the file you wish to undelete.

DOS Shell Users: Use the **Disk Utilities, Undelete** command.

The RENAME Command

The REN command is used to rename files. As an example, let us assume that we want to rename a file on the disc in the logged drive from its current filename OLDFILE.DOC to the new filename NEWFILE.DOC. This can be done as follows:

```
C>REN OLDFILE.DOC NEWFILE.DOC
```

Note the importance of spaces after REN and in between the two file names. The command can be interpreted as:

```
Rename from filename1 to filename2
```

To rename a file on a disc in a disc drive other than the logged drive, the disc drive specification must also be included in the command, as follows:

```
C>REN A:OLDFILE.DOC NEWFILE.DOC
```

Note that, if you intend to rename a file and give it a filename that already exists on disc, you must first delete the unwanted file before renaming, otherwise MS-DOS will refuse to obey your command.

DOS Shell Users: First select the file you want to rename, then use the **File, Rename** command.

The CHKDSK & SCANDISK Commands

CHKDSK is the disc-checking program found in all pre-DOS 6.2 versions. In MS-DOS 6.2 the command has been replaced by SCANDISK which works on both compressed and uncompressed drives and, in fact, offers much more than CHKDSK.

Each disc has a file-allocation table (FAT) where a note is kept of which clusters have been allocated to which file. However, with heavy disc use, the file-allocation table can be corrupted and using CHKDSK will report 'lost clusters found'. The /f switch, allows CHKDSK to also do some routine maintenance, namely fixing lost clusters. A cluster is the minimum amount of space (one or more sectors) than can be allocated to a file on disc. The /f switch converts these into files and gives them the general name FILExxxx.CHK, where xxxx starts with 0000 and increments by 1. These files can then be checked and perhaps deleted if found to be useless.

The command takes the form:

```
C>CHKDSK /F
```

which checks the disc in the logged drive.

SCANDISK, like CHKDSK can detect cross links, but it can also repair the files corrupted by cross linking in the data structure of both compressed and uncompressed discs. The program checks the 'Media descriptor', the 'File allocation tables', the 'Directory structure', the 'File system', and performs a 'Surface scan'. To run the program, type SCANDISK at the command prompt.

The XCOPY Command

The XCOPY command allows us to copy files and directories, including lower level sub-directories, if they exist (see following section for a full explanation of these), to the specified destination drive and directory. The command takes the following form:

    C>XCOPY source_filespec destination [switches]

where *source_filespec* specifies the source file or drive and directory you want to copy and *destination* can be the drive to which you want this source file to be copied. For example,

    C>**XCOPY A:*.* B:**

will copy all files in the A: drive to the B: drive. If you only have one floppy drive, you will be prompted to change discs.

Some of the *options* available (for a full list see the 'Command Summary' section) are as follows:

/d	copies source files which were modified on or after a specified date
/p	prompts the user with '(Y/N?)' before copying files
/s	copies directories and their sub-directories unless they are empty
/v	causes verification of each file as it is written.

XCOPY copies all files and subdirectories in the specified directory (except hidden and system files) from one disc to another by reading from the source disc as many files as possible into memory, then copying them to the target disc. This is unlike the COPY command which copies each file in turn, therefore, taking much longer. However, when the target disc becomes full, XCOPY stops and does not ask for another disc to be inserted in the target drive.

XCOPY can copy files even when the two discs are of different format, unlike the DISKCOPY command which requires that the source and target disc be the same format.

3. THE DIRECTORY TREE

If you are using a system with low-capacity disc drives, then organising the files you keep on discs is relatively straightforward. The usual method would be to keep similar applications on the same disc, so that one disc might contain files on word processing, another on spreadsheets, and another on databases. MS-DOS keeps track of all such files by allocating space on each disc, called a directory, in which such information as the name of each file, its size, the date it was last amended, etc., is kept.

However, as you move up to systems with high-capacity disc drives (1.2 or 1.44 Mbyte floppies) and especially to systems with hard discs of 50, 100, 150 or more Mbytes, the amount of information you can store on them increases so much, that unless you organise the way you keep your files on such discs, you could easily spend all of your available time trying to find one.

MS-DOS can help you to organise your files on disc by providing a system of directories and subdirectories. The key to the MS-DOS system is the 'root' directory, indicated by the back-slash sign (\), which is the main directory under which a number of subdirectories can be created. In turn, each subdirectory can have its own subdirectories, as shown below.

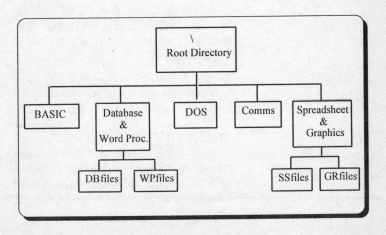

The root directory is shown here with five subdirectories under it, while two of these have their own subdirectories below them. For maximum efficiency, the root directory should contain only the System and start-up files, together with information on its subdirectories, a kind of an index drawer to a filing system.

Files in different subdirectories can have the same name because MS-DOS can be told which is which via a system of PATH names. For example, a file in the SSFILES subdirectory could have the same name, say SALARY.TMP, as one in the GRFILES subdirectory. Nevertheless, we can instruct MS-DOS to fetch the file in the SSFILES subdirectory by giving its path name which is:

    \SPREADSH\SSFILES\SALARY.TMP

whereas that of the file in the GRFILES subdirectory is:

    \SPREADSH\GRFILES\SALARY.TMP

In the example shown previously, the contents of the various subdirectories might be as follows:

\   The root directory, containing the two
                        hidden System files MSDOS.SYS and
                        IO.SYS, the Command Processor
                        COMMAND.COM, the CONFIG.SYS
                        file, the AUTOEXEC.BAT file, the
                        names of all its subdirectories (five in
                        our example).

BASIC   A subdirectory containing all the
                        QBASIC programs which came with
                        version 5 and 6 of DOS, such as
                        QBASIC.EXE and the help file
                        QBASIC.HLP and any programs you
                        write in QuickBasic which will have
                        the .BAS extension. Earlier versions
                        of DOS have different versions of
                        BASIC, such as BASICA or
                        GWBASIC.

| DATABASE | A subdirectory containing a database with built-in word processor. Below this, there are two subdirectories; one for the database files (DBfiles), and one for the word processor files (WPfiles). The actual files in these subdirectories could have extensions which depend on the software. |

| DOS | A subdirectory containing all the MS-DOS files comprising the external MS-DOS commands. |

| COMMS | A subdirectory containing communications programs, proprietary back-up software, etc. |

| SPREADSH | A subdirectory containing an integrated spreadsheet and graphics package. Below this, there are two sub-directories, one for the spread sheet files (SSfiles), and one for the graphics files (GRfiles). Again, the actual files in these could have different extensions which might be a function of the software package. |

The Directory Listing

You could create the above directories with their sub-directories on your hard disc, but you might follow our example and set-up these on a floppy disc to avoid changing the configuration of your hard disc. Had you done so, typing the command DIR, displays what is shown on the next page.

The volume name (given on the display as MS-DOS_6) might be different in your case, as it depends on the label you gave your disc just after formatting. If you did not give a disc a label, then that line will read 'Volume in drive A has no label', assuming, of course, that you are accessing the A: drive.

```
C:\>dir a:

 Volume in drive A is MS-DOS_6
 Directory of A:\

COMMAND  COM        54,619 30/09/93    6:20
AUTOEXEC BAT          640 09/11/93   19:42
CONFIG   SYS          361 09/11/93   19:42
BASIC         <DIR>       11/11/93   22:11
DATABASE      <DIR>       11/11/93   22:13
DOS           <DIR>       11/11/93   22:15
COMMS         <DIR>       11/11/93   22:16
SPREADSH      <DIR>       11/11/93   22:17
        8 file(s)        55,620 bytes
                        662,528 bytes free

C:\>
```

The second line of the display depends on your system and you have no control over it. Note that directories are distinguished from files in the directory listing by the inclusion of the letters <DIR> (in angled brackets) against their name. The order of their appearance depends on the order of their creation.

These days, many program packages create their own directory structure during installation and suggest names for the required directories and subdirectories into which they deposit their files. What they don't usually do, is to create subdirectories for your data. These you must create yourself in order to avoid adding your data files into the same directory as the one holding the program files. Doing so, makes it easier for you to make a back-up of your data files onto floppy discs, makes future upgrading of your programs easier and lays the foundation for a structured hard-disc system.

The TREE Command:

MS-DOS contains a very useful external command called 'tree'. Its use allows you to see pictorially the way DOS structures directories and subdirectories, as shown on the next page.

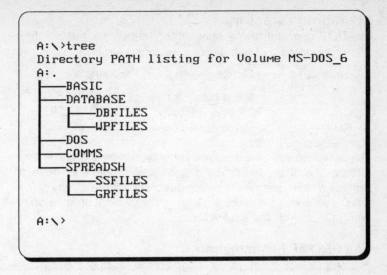

```
A:\>tree
Directory PATH listing for Volume MS-DOS_6
A:.
├───BASIC
├───DATABASE
│   ├───DBFILES
│   └───WPFILES
├───DOS
├───COMMS
└───SPREADSH
    ├───SSFILES
    └───GRFILES

A:\>
```

In versions of MS-DOS prior to version 4, this command produces only a character listing of directories and sub-directories, as opposed to the graphical visualisation which was introduced with the DOS version 4.0 and carried forward to later versions of the operating system.

The topmost level in a disc directory structure is the root directory which is created automatically by MS-DOS when you format a new disc and, unlike other directories, it does not have a unique name. It is within the root directory that you can create additional directories and subdirectories and give them unique names.

When you create directories and subdirectories, MS-DOS creates what is known as the dot (.) and double dot (..) entries. These shorthand notations can be used to identify the current and the parent directory, respectively. Thus, typing

    DIR ..

at the DOS System prompt, lists the files in the parent directory of the current subdirectory on the logged disc drive.

Managing Directories

MS-DOS provides three special commands for the creation and management of sub-directories. these are:

Command	Meaning	Example
MD	Make subdirectory	C>MD \BASIC
CD	Change directory	C>CD \BASIC
RD	Remove directory	C>RD \BASIC

These will be explained in detail shortly, but before we go any further, it will be extremely useful and prudent to have a prompt which indicates in which directory we are at any given time. We can do this by changing the prompt from always being C>, to indicate the PATH.

The PROMPT Command:

A prompt which displays the logged directory is of the form:

```
C:\>_
```

indicating that the current directory is the root directory, shown by the back-slash (\). From this point on, the DOS prompt will be included at the beginning of each command. DO NOT TYPE THESE PROMPTS, they should be already on the screen. Having a prompt which indicates in which directory we are at any given time is imperative because without it you could be copying files to the wrong subdirectory without realising it.

If your system is already configured, then an appropriate entry will exist within your AUTOEXEC.BAT file (discussed in Chapter 5) which produces this form of prompt. However, if it is not the case, then type

```
C>PROMPT $P$G
```

and press <Enter>.

To insert the pg command in your AUTOEXEC.BAT file, you will need to learn to use either the **Edit** screen editor (available to users of MS-DOS versions 5 & 6, and to be discussed in Chapter 4) or the **Edlin** line editor (available to users of pre-DOS 5 versions, and discussed in Appendix B). Alternatively, you could use any other editor or word processor, provided it can save files in text (ASCII) format.

32

Creating a Directory:

Before a directory can be used, it must exist. If it does not, you can make it with the MD command. To make the subdirectory to the root directory, called BASIC, so that you could transfer to it all BASIC programs and files from your DOS subdirectory, type the following line

```
C:\>MD\BASIC
```

which makes the BASIC subdirectory in the root directory of the C: drive, and waits for further commands.

If you wanted to create this subdirectory on the A: drive, then you should have changed the logged drive first by typing

```
C:\>A:
A:\>_
```

and then issue the 'make directory' command.

In our example, the full path was given after the MD command, by first specifying the root directory with the use of the back-slash (\), followed by the name of the subdirectory.

To transfer files from the DOS subdirectory, first change directory using the CD command so that the logged directory is the target directory to which you will be copying the files, by typing

```
C:\>CD\BASIC
C:\BASIC>_
```

which causes the prompt to change, indicating that MS-DOS has actually changed directory. Without the prompt change, you would have had the typical 'where am I?' problem. Note that the moment we create a subdirectory we tend to refer to its parent as directory, even though itself might be a subdirectory to another parent directory.

To copy all BASIC programs and files from the \DOS directory, to this new \BASIC directory, type

```
C:\BASIC>COPY C:\DOS\QBAS*.*
```

Alternatively, we could have issued these commands from the root directory without first changing directories. In this case, the previous command would have to be typed as

```
C:\>COPY C:\DOS\QBAS*.* C:\BASIC
```

The first form of the COPY command says 'copy all files whose names start with QBAS from the \DOS directory to the logged directory', while the second form of the command says 'copy all files whose names start with QBAS from the \DOS directory to the \BASIC directory'.

Renaming Directories

Should you be dissatisfied with the name of an existing directory and you want to rename it, you can do so easily enough if you are a DOS 6 user. Pre-DOS 6 users must follow the slightly more complicated procedure, listed below.

DOS 6 Users

Use the **move** command. To find out everything there is to know about this command, type

```
C:\>MOVE /?
```

or

```
C:|>HELP MOVE
```

Pre-DOS 6 Users

- Create another directory, giving it your preferred name,
- Copy to the newly created directory all the files from the unwanted directory,
- Delete all files from the unwanted directory,
- Remove the unwanted directory from its parent directory.

This procedure is essential because:

(a)   Prior to MS-DOS 6 you could not rename directories from the system prompt,

(b)   you could not remove directories unless they were empty.

As an example of the above procedure (whether you are a DOS 6 user or not, let us assume that we have created, as discussed previously, a subdirectory to the root directory, called DATA. To have created such a subdirectory, we would have had to return to the root directory from whichever subdirectory we were in at the time, by typing

```
CD \
```

at the DOS System prompt.
   We now proceed to create a subdirectory to the DATA directory, called DOCS, by first changing directory from the root directory to that of DATA, as follows:

```
C:\>CD \DATA
C:\DATA>_
```

then make a subdirectory called DOCS by typing

```
C:\DATA>MD DOCS
```

at the prompt.
   Note that we have not placed a back-slash in front of the new subdirectory name which causes it to be made in the currently logged directory. Had we included the back-slash, the subdirectory DOCS would have been created as a subdirectory of the root directory.
   Alternatively, we could make DOCS without first changing directory by issuing the MD command from the root directory, but giving the full path specification. Having made the subdirectory DOCS, copy into it your files, as discussed previously.
   Let us now assume that for some reason the directory name DOCS offends you and you would like to change it to WPDOCS instead. To do this you will have to type in the following commands, assuming you are at the root directory of the C: drive:

DOS 6 users

Type the following command:

```
C:\>MOVE C:\DATA\DOCS C:\DATA\WPDOCS
```

the message c:\data\docs => c:\data\wpdocs [ok] confirms successful renaming.

Pre-DOS 6 users

Type the following commands:

```
C:\>CD \DATA
C:\DATA>MD WPDOCS
C:\DATA>COPY DOCS\*.* WPDOCS
C:\DATA>DEL DOCS\*.*
Are you sure? (Y/N)Y
C:\DATA>RD DOCS
C:\DATA>_
```

In order of appearance, these commands do the following:

(a)   changes directory to DATA
(b)   makes a subdirectory called WPDOCS
(c)   copies from subdirectory DOCS all files to sub-directory WPDOCS
(d)   deletes all files from the DOCS subdirectory
(e)   MS-DOS asks for confirmation
(f)   removes subdirectory DOCS.

Thus, restructuring directories, moving files from one directory to another, or making back-ups of groups of files, is much easier with DOS 6, or with the use of the DOS Shell. However, the DOS Shell is only available to users of DOS version 4 & 5.

As you can see, renaming directories if you are a pre-DOS 4 user is cumbersome, so think how you want to structure your hard disc before plunging into it blindly. However, life can be made easier with the use of certain proprietary software, such as Symantec's Norton Commander, or Central Point's PC Tools to name but two.

4. THE MS-DOS EDITOR

Users of MS-DOS version 5 and 6 are provided with a full screen editor, called **Edit**, with which special ASCII files can be created that customise your system. These are text files which, when sent to the screen or printer, are interpreted as text, unlike the .COM or .EXE files which are binary files.

Edit can also be used to create the source code of various programming languages, such as Fortran and C. In such cases, do remember to give the files the appropriate extension, which for the two languages mentioned, are **.for** and **.c**, respectively.

To invoke **Edit**, the disc that contains it must be accessible and the full path of the file you want to create or edit must be specified. Thus, typing the command:

    C:\>edit test.txt

expects to find both **Edit** and the fictitious file **test.txt** on the disc in the logged drive (in this case C:) or on the system PATH, while typing

    C:\>edit A:test.txt

expects to find **Edit** on the C: drive, and the file **test.txt** on the disc in the A: drive.

If the file does not exist on the specified disc or directory, then **Edit** displays a blank screen, as follows:

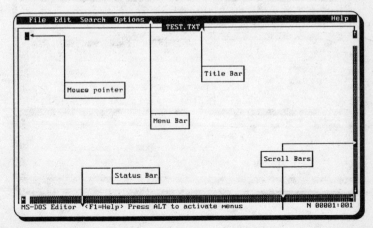

The **Edit** screen is subdivided into several areas which have the following function:

Area	Function
Menu bar	allows you to choose from several main menu options
Title bar	displays the name of the current file. If a new file, it displays the word <Untitled>
Status bar	displays the current file status and information regarding the present process
Scroll bar	allows you to scroll the screen with the use of the mouse.

The area bounded by the Title bar and the two Scroll bars is known as the view window. It is in this area that you enter the contents of a new file or load and view the contents of an old file.

The **Edit** screen can also be invoked from within DOS Shell by selecting the **Editor** from the Main group of programs, as shown below:

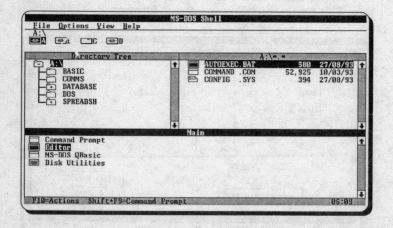

On starting **Edit**, the dialogue box shown below appears in the middle of the screen asking you to type in the name of the file you want to edit. Type **test.txt** and either click the **OK** button in the dialogue box, or press the <Enter> key.

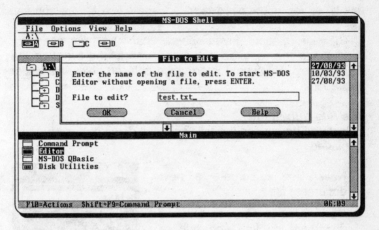

The Editor Menu Bar

Each menu bar option on the editor, has associated with it a pull-down sub-menu. To activate the menu bar, either press the <Alt> key, which causes the first item on the menu bar (in this case **File**) to be highlighted, then use the right and left arrow keys to highlight any of the items of the menu bar, or use the mouse to point to an item. Pressing either the <Enter> key, or the left mouse button, reveals the pull-down sub-menu of the highlighted menu item.

The pull-down sub-menus can also be activated directly by pressing the <Alt> key followed by the first letter of the required menu option. Thus pressing <Alt+O>, causes the **Options** sub-menu to be displayed. Use the up and down arrow keys to move the highlighted bar up and down within a sub-menu, or the right and left arrow keys to move along the options of the menu bar. Pressing the <Enter> key selects the highlighted option, while pressing the <Esc> key closes the menu system.

The Menu Bar Options:

Each item of the menu bar offers the options described below. However, dimmed command names in the **Edit** sub-menu indicate that these commands are unavailable at this time; you might need to select some text before you can use them.

The information given below can be displayed by highlighting the required sub-menu option and pressing the **F1** help key. This same information is listed below for easier reference.

The File Sub-Menu

Selecting **File** causes the following pull-down sub-menu to be displayed:

New: Use to create a new document file.

Open: Use to open an existing document so you can edit or print it.

Save: Use to save the current version of your document.

Save As: Use to save your document as a file. To preserve the previous version of your document, rename it in the File Name dialogue box.

Print: Use to print all or part of a document.

Exit: Use to quit the MS-DOS Editor environment.

The Edit Sub-Menu

Selecting **Edit** causes the following pull-down sub-menu to be displayed:

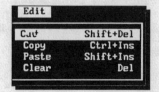

Cut: Use to remove selected text and put it on the Clipboard, a temporary holding area.

Copy: Use to copy selected text to the Clipboard. The original text remains unchanged.

Paste: Use to insert a block of text from the Clipboard at any point in a document.

Clear: Use to delete selected text without copying it to the Clipboard. The Clipboard's contents remain unchanged.

The Search Sub-Menu
Selecting **Search** causes the following pull-down sub-menu to be displayed:

Find: Use to search for a text string. You can request a case-sensitive match or a whole-word match.

Repeat Last Find: Use to repeat the search performed by the most recent Find or Change command.

Change: Use to replace one text string with another.

The Options Sub-Menu
Selecting **Options** causes the following pull-down sub-menu to be displayed:

Display: Use to control screen colour, scroll bars in windows, and the number of spaces the <Tab> key advances the cursor.

Help Path: Use to change the directories that the MS-DOS Editor searches to find the Help file EDIT.HLP

Help Menu
Selecting **Help** causes the following pull-down sub-menu to be displayed:

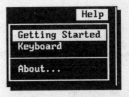

Getting Started: Use to find out about using MS-DOS Editor

menus, commands, and dialogue boxes. Also to get Help on using the Editor and using options when starting the program.

Keyboard: Use to find out about keystrokes for performing tasks on the MS-DOS Editor, and the WordStar keystrokes that can be used with it.

About: Use to display the version number and copyright information for the MS-DOS Editor.

Dialogue Boxes:

Three periods after a sub-menu option, means that a dialogue box will open when the option is selected. A dialogue box is used for the insertion of additional information, such as the name of a file to be opened, or to be acted upon in some way.

To understand dialogue boxes, type the word 'hi' in the edit screen, then press **Alt+S**, and select the **Change** option from the revealed sub-menu of **Search**. The dialogue box shown below will now appear on the screen.

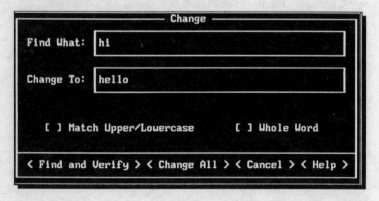

The <Tab> key can be used to move the cursor from one field to another within a dialogue box, while the <Enter> key is only used to indicate that the options within the various fields within the dialogue box are specified correctly. Every dialogue box contains one field which is enclosed in emboldened angle-brackets (<Find and Verify>, in the above example). This field indicates the action that **Edit** will take if the <Enter> key is pressed (in our example, the word 'hi' will be changed to 'hello', if this is what we choose to type against the 'Find What' and 'Change To' fields. Pressing the <Esc> key aborts the menu option and returns you to the editor.

The cursor can be moved to any part of the text being typed in the view window, and corrections can be made, with the use of the key strokes described below.

Key	Function
←	moves the cursor to the left by one character.
→	moves the cursor to the right by one character.
Ctrl+←	moves the cursor to the beginning of the previous word on the current line.
Ctrl+→	moves the cursor to the beginning of the next word on the current line.
Home	moves the cursor to the first column of the current line.
End	moves the cursor to the end of the last word on the current line.
↑	moves the cursor up one line.
↓	moves the cursor down one line.
Ctrl+Home	moves the cursor to the first line of the current screen.
Ctrl+End	moves the cursor to the last line of the current screen.
PgUp	moves the cursor to the previous screen.
PgDn	moves the cursor to the next screen.

Ctrl+PgUp	moves the cursor left one screen.
Ctrl+PgDn	moves the cursor right one screen.
Ins	toggles the Insert mode from ON (its default position) to OFF and back again.
Enter	moves the cursor to the beginning of the next line, provided the insert mode is in the ON position.
Ctrl+Y	deletes the line at the current cursor position.
Ctrl+N	inserts a blank line at the current cursor position.
Shift+Arrows	(any one of ←↑→↓ arrow keys) marks block areas on the screen to be used with the sub-menu of the Edit option, namely Cut, Copy, Paste, and Clear.

When areas of text are marked, with either the use of the <Shift+Arrows> or by clicking and dragging the mouse, the **Edit**, **Cut** and **Copy** options store the contents of the blocked (highlighted) area of text in a temporary storage area known as the 'Clipboard' from which it can be retrieved later when the **Paste** option is used. The Clipboard stores only one block of information at a time. If you attempt to store a second block of information, it simply overrides the previously stored block.

If you are not using a mouse, you might want to clear the scroll bars from the screen, to give you more room. This can be done by pressing <Alt+O>, selecting the **Display** option and pressing the <Tab> key until the cursor is positioned in the 'Scroll Bars' field. Pressing the spacebar toggles the option into the off position by clearing the letter X from within the square brackets.

If you are using a mouse, scrolling text in the view window is easy. Place the mouse pointer on the top, bottom, left or right of the scroll bars and click the left mouse button to scroll upwards, downwards, to the left or to the right, respectively.

There are a lot more commands associated with **Edit**, but you'll find that the ones given above are sufficient for almost all your needs.

Creating & Saving a Text File

As an example, type the following four lines in **Edit**'s view window, pressing the <Enter> key at the end of each line.

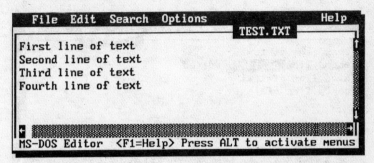

Editing Text:

To edit any part of the document, use the up or down arrow keys to place the cursor at the beginning of the line you want to edit, then use the right or left arrow keys to place the cursor at the required position where you want to begin editing.

If you have a mouse, simply point to the place you want to edit and click the left mouse button to place the cursor at the position occupied by the mouse pointer.

Use one of the above techniques to change the second line of our document to

```
Second line of text, edited
```

Selecting Text:

To select text with the keyboard, place the cursor at the required starting position, and while holding down the <Shift> key, press the right or left arrow keys to highlight as much of the text on that line as you like.

To select text with the mouse, place the mouse pointer at the required starting position and while holding down the left mouse button, move the mouse horizontally to the right or left to highlight the required text on that line. If you try to select text which runs to more than one line, the whole line (first and subsequent) will be selected. Thus, you can either select text from part of a line, or you select text from whole lines.

As an example, select the words ' of text' (including the leading space) from the second line, as shown below:

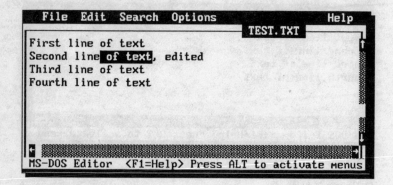

Moving Text:

Having selected the part of text you want to move, use the **Edit, Cut** command, then place the cursor at the required point where you would like to move the text to, and use the **Edit, Paste** command. In our example, move the selected text to the end of the fourth line. The result is shown below:

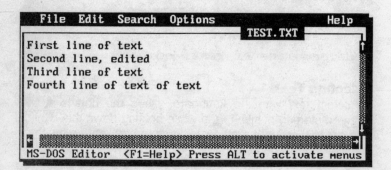

Clearing Text:

To remove text from a document without changing the contents of the Clipboard, highlight the unwanted text, then use the **Edit, Clear** command.

Use this command to remove from the fourth line both repetitions of the words 'of text', then, to prove that the contents of the Clipboard have not changed, use the **Edit, Paste** command to restore the fourth line to its original form.

In fact, you can paste the contents of the Clipboard to any part of a document, as many times as you like, because pasting does not empty the Clipboard.

Copying Text:

To copy text, highlight the required text, then use the **Edit, Copy** command.

Use this command to copy the whole of the second line to the Clipboard, then use the **Edit, Paste** command, to paste a copy of it on to the fifth line of the document. Next, change the words 'Second' to 'Fifth' and 'edited' to 'added', as shown below.

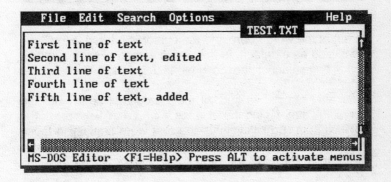

You will have to use the <Del> key to delete the unwanted words as the editor is normally in 'insert' mode and when typing text it inserts it at the cursor position. To toggle the edit mode from 'insert' to 'overtype', press the <Ins> key once.

Finding Text:

To find a specific word or part of a word, use the **Search, Find** command which causes the following dialogue box to appear on your screen:

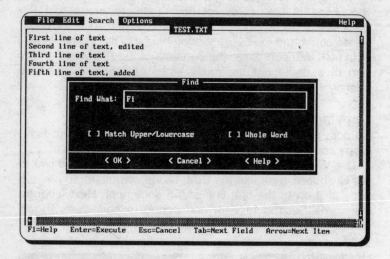

Note that the word nearest to the cursor is offered in the 'Find What' field as a default. In the above example, if the cursor is at the beginning of the document, the default word will be 'First'.

As an example, to find all the words that begin with the letters 'Fi', after typing these in the 'Find What' field, press the <OK> button. **Edit** highlights the first word containing these letters, and to find the next occurrence you will have to use the **Search, Repeat Last Find** command, or press **F3**.

Saving a Document:

To save a document that you have already named, use the **File, Save** command. To save an unnamed document, or to save it under a different name, use the **File, Save As** command which causes the dialogue box, shown on the next page, to appear on your screen.

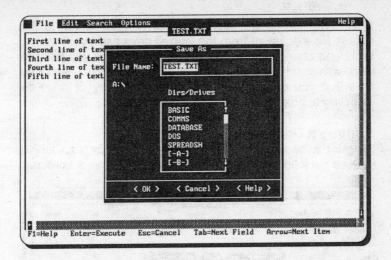

Note that you can save a document to any subdirectory or drive by selecting appropriately from the Dirs/Drives list within the dialogue box.

Opening a Document:

Once a document has been saved to a file on disc, you can open it by using the **File, Open** command which causes the dialogue box shown below to appear on your screen.

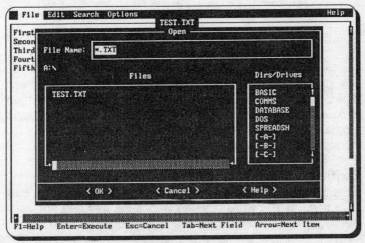

Again, you can select any of the .TXT files (which is the default file extension) from the logged drive and subdirectory, or indeed change the extension to, say, .BAT if you want to work with batch files such as the AUTOEXEC.BAT file Also note that you can change the logged directory or drive by selecting appropriately from the Dirs/Drives list.

Printing a Document:

To print a document, use the **File, Print** command which causes the following dialogue box to appear on your screen.

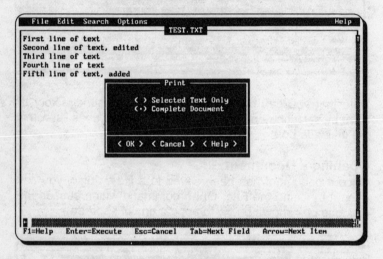

You can choose to print the complete document (the default setting), or a pre-selected part of it. If you are printing the whole document, simply press the **<OK>** button, but if you are printing a selected part of it (which must have been selected before initiating the **File, Print** command), then choose the 'Selected Text Only' option. The **Print** command works only if you have a printer connected to or redirected through your parallel printer port (LPT1).

Exiting the Editor

To end the current session and exit **Edit**, select the **File, Exit** command. If you were working with a file that had not been saved, **Edit** will prompt you to save it before exiting.

5. SYSTEM CONFIGURATION

The CONFIG.SYS File

This file allows you to configure your computer to your needs, as commands held in it are executed during booting up the system. The easiest way to amend this system file is with the use of **Edit**, as discussed in the previous chapter, provided of course you are running under DOS version 5 or 6. Pre-DOS 5 users will have to use **Edlin** (see Appendix B).

If you are setting up your system for the first time, and depending on what version of DOS you are using, you might need to change the CONFIG.SYS file that is created for you by the SETUP program, because it might not include all the commands you will require to run your system efficiently. If your system had already been running under an earlier version of DOS, then the SETUP program might have added some extra commands to your CONFIG.SYS file. You might also need to change some of the CONFIG.SYS file commands to optimise your system.

If your system has been implemented by, say, your computer staff, do not edit this file or use **Edit** to look at its contents, unless you have to and you know precisely what you are doing, as the file contains entries that MS-DOS uses to define specific operating attributes. To view the contents of the file, use the TYPE command at the system prompt.

DOS Shell Users: To view the contents of a file, select it, then use the **File, View File Contents** command.

Some possible contents of CONFIG.SYS in a pre-DOS 5 version, as well as those for a DOS 5 and 6 implementation, are shown below. The list following these two examples, contains commands that you can include within the CONFIG.SYS file.

Do remember, however, that any changes made to the CONFIG.SYS file only take effect after you reboot your system, which can be achieved by pressing the 3 keys <Ctrl+Alt+Del> simultaneously.

Pre-DOS 5 Users:

Use the **Edlin** line editor to amend your CONFIG.SYS file so as to include the following commands:

```
1:*FILES=20
2:*BUFFERS=30
3:*BREAK=ON
4:*COUNTRY=044
5:*DEVICE=C:\DOS\ANSI.SYS
```

Users of MS/PC-DOS 3.3 or 4.01, should substitute the following COUNTRY= entry

```
COUNTRY=044,437,C:\DOS\COUNTRY.SYS
```

for the one given above. It is understood, of course, that your particular CONFIG.SYS file might contain additional entries.

DOS 5 or 6 Users:

Use the **Edit** screen editor to amend your CONFIG.SYS file so as to include the commands shown below. Again, it is more than likely that your CONFIG.SYS file will include different commands to those shown below.

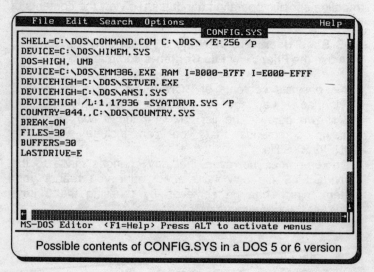

```
  File  Edit  Search  Options                        Help
                              CONFIG.SYS
SHELL=C:\DOS\COMMAND.COM C:\DOS\ /E:256 /p
DEVICE=C:\DOS\HIMEM.SYS
DOS=HIGH, UMB
DEVICE=C:\DOS\EMM386.EXE RAM I=B000-B7FF I=E000-EFFF
DEVICEHIGH=C:\DOS\SETVER.EXE
DEVICEHIGH=C:\DOS\ANSI.SYS
DEVICEHIGH /L:1,17936 =SYATDRVR.SYS /P
COUNTRY=044,,C:\DOS\COUNTRY.SYS
BREAK=ON
FILES=30
BUFFERS=30
LASTDRIVE=E




MS-DOS Editor  <F1=Help> Press ALT to activate menus
```

Possible contents of CONFIG.SYS in a DOS 5 or 6 version

For example, if you are not running a computer with a 386 or higher processor, then the 4th line (the one with EMM386.EXE) will not, and should not, be included.

As seen above, under DOS 5 and 6, you can take advantage of high memory to load DOS and some device drivers into it, thus saving conventional memory.

Configuration Commands:

A brief explanation of the configuration commands, which can be included within the CONFIG.SYS file is given below.

BREAK

By including the command BREAK=ON in the CONFIG.SYS file, you can use of the key combination <Ctrl+C> or <Ctrl+Break> to interrupt DOS I/O functions.

BUFFERS

DOS allocates memory space in RAM, called buffers, to store whole sectors of data being read from disc, each of 512 bytes in size. If more data are required, MS-DOS first searches the buffers before searching the disc, which speeds up operations. The number of buffers can be changed by using:

BUFFERS=n

where n can be a number from 1 to 99.

However, as each buffer requires an additional 0.5 Kbyte of RAM, the number you should use is dependent on the relative size between the package you are using and your computer's RAM. Best results are obtained by choosing between 10-30 buffers.

CODEPAGE   This command is to be found in
MS/PC-DOS versions 3.3 and 4.01.
The table that DOS uses to define a
character set is called a code page.
Thus, include the command

CODEPAGE=437

where 437 is the code page definition
of pre-DOS 3.3 versions.

COUNTRY   MS-DOS displays dates according to
the US format which is
month/day/year. To change this to
day/month/year, use the command

COUNTRY=044

where 044 is for UK users. Non UK
users can substitute their international
telephone country code for the 044.
The default value is 001, for the USA.

Users of DOS 3.3 or higher, should
enter this statement as

COUNTRY=044,,C:\DOS\COUNTRY.SYS

assuming that COUNTRY.SYS is to
be found in the \DOS subdirectory.

DEVICE   DOS includes its own standard device
drivers which allow communication
with your keyboard, screen and discs.
Such drivers can be extended to allow
other devices to be connected by
specifying them in the CONFIG.SYS
file. Example of these are:

DEVICE=ANSI.SYS

which loads alternative screen and
keyboard drivers for ANSI support -
features of which are required by
some commercial software.

DEVICE=SETVER.EXE

which sets the DOS version number that MS-DOS versions 5 and 6 reports to a program. You can use the SETVER command at the prompt to display the version table, which lists names of programs and the number of the MS-DOS version with which they are designed to run, or add a program that has not been updated to MS-DOS 5 or 6.

DEVICE=MOUSEAnn.SYS

allows the use of specific mouse devices.

DEVICE=VDISK.SYS n

allows you to specify the size n in Kbytes (default 64) of RAM to be used as an extra very fast virtual disc. With computers which have more than 640 Kbytes of RAM, the option /E can be used after n to allocate the specified memory size from the extra area of RAM.

DEVICE=DRIVER.SYS

allows you to connect an external disc drive.

DEVICE=EGA.SYS

provides mouse support for EGA modes.

DEVICE=COMn.SYS

specifies asynchronous drivers for the serial ports, where n=01 specifies an IBM PC AT COM device, and n=02 specifies an IBM PS/2 COM device.

DEVICEHIGH	Loads device drivers into the upper memory area under DOS 5 and 6.
DOS	Sets the area of RAM where DOS 5 and 6 will be located, and specifies whether to use the upper memory area. The command takes the form: DOS=HIGH
DRIVPARM	Sets characteristics of a disc drive under DOS 5 and 6.
FCBS	Specifies the number of FCBs (File Control Blocks) that can be opened concurrently. The command takes the form: FCBS=x,y where x is the number of files that can be opened at any one time (from 1 to 255, with a default value of 4), and y is the number of opened files (from 1-255) that cannot be closed automatically by DOS if an application tries to open more than x files.
FILES	DOS normally allows 8 files to be opened at a time. However, some software such as relational databases, might require to refer to more files at any given time. To accommodate this, DOS allows you to change this default value by using: FILES=n where n can be a number from 8 to the maximum required by your application which typically could be 30, although the maximum allowable is 255 (99 in DOS 5).

| INCLUDE | New to DOS 6 - it includes the contents of one configuration block within another. This command can be used only within a menu block in your CONFIG.SYS file. |

| INSTALL | This command runs a terminate-and-stay-resident (TSR) program, such as FASTOPEN, KEYB, NLSFUNC, or SHARE when MS-DOS reads the CONFIG.SYS file. The command is available under DOS 4.01 or higher, and takes the following form: |

INSTALL=filespec[params]

where *params* specifies the optional line to pass to the *filespec* which must be FASTOPEN.EXE, KEYB.EXE, NLSFUNC.EXE or SHARE.EXE.

| LASTDRIVE | This command is used if additional drives are to be connected to your system, or you are sharing a hard disc on a network. The command takes the form: |

LASTDRIVE=x

where x is a letter from A to Z (default E).

| MENUCOLOR | New to MS-DOS 6 - it sets the text and background colours for the start-up menu. This command can be used only within a menu block in your CONFIG.SYS file. |

| MENUDEFAULT | New to MS-DOS 6 - it specifies the default menu item on the start-up menu and sets a time-out value. This command can be used only within a menu block in your CONFIG.SYS file. |

MENUITEM	New to MS-DOS 6 - it defines up to nine items on the start-up menu. This command can be used only within a menu block in your CONFIG.SYS file.
NUMLOCK	New to MS-DOS 6 - NUMLOCK=OFF (or ON) controls initial setting of the <NumLock> key. This command can only be used within a menu block in your CONFIG.SYS file.
REM	REM followed by any string, allows remarks to be entered in the CONFIG.SYS. A semicolon (;) at the beginning of a line has the same effect.
SET	Displays, sets or removes DOS environment variables. This command can be used in your CONFIG.SYS, your AUTOEXEC.BAT, or at the command prompt.
SHELL	Manufacturers of some PCs provide a 'front end' or an alternative Command Processor to COMMAND.COM as real-mode command-line processor. To invoke this, the command SHELL must be included within the CONFIG.SYS file. The command takes the form:

SHELL=FRONTEND.COM

where FRONTEND is the name of the alternative Command Processor. The default value of SHELL is COMMAND.COM.

STACKS	Sets the amount of RAM that DOS 5 and 6 reserves for processing hardware interrupts.

SUBMENU	New to MS-DOS 6 - it defines an item on a start-up menu. This command can be used only within a menu block in your CONFIG.SYS file.
SWITCHES	Specifies the use of conventional keyboard functions even though an enhanced keyboard is installed. The command is only available under DOS 5 and 6.
VERIFY	Forces DOS to verify that files are written correctly to disc. The command can also be used at the command prompt.

For multiple configurations under DOS 6, refer to the second half of the next chapter.

The COMMAND.COM Processor

This command starts a new command processor that contains all internal commands. This is loaded into memory in two parts: the resident part and the transient part which can be overwritten by some programs in which case the resident part can be used to reload the transient part. The command takes the form:

    COMMAND [options]

with the following available options:

/E specifies the environment size in bytes, with a default value of 160 bytes

/P prohibits COMMAND.COM from exiting to a higher level

/C executes a following command.

For example, the following statement

`C:\>COMMAND /C CHKDSK A:`

which might appear in a program starts a new command processor under the current program, runs the CHKDSK command on the disc in the A: drive, and returns to the first command processor. DOS 6 users should not use the CHKDSK utility, but should use the much superior SCANDISK utility.

The AUTOEXEC.BAT File

This is a special batch file that DOS looks for during the last stages of booting up and if it exists, the commands held in it are executed. One such command is the KEYB xx which configures keyboards for the appropriate national standard, with xx indicating the country. For the UK, the command becomes KEYB UK, and you will need to execute it if your keyboard is marked with the double quotes sign on the 2 key and/or the @ sign over the single quotes key.

The easiest way to amend this system file, as with any text file, is with the use of **Edit** (or **Edlin** for pre-DOS 5 users), as discussed earlier.

If you are setting up your system for the first time you might need to change the AUTOEXEC.BAT file that was created for you by the SETUP program, because it might not include all the commands you will require to run your system efficiently. If your system had already been running under an earlier version of DOS, then the SETUP program might have added some extra commands to your AUTOEXEC.BAT file. You might need to change some of the AUTOEXEC.BAT file commands to optimise your system, or to automatically start up an application program or utility.

Some of the possible contents of AUTOEXEC.BAT in a pre-DOS 5 version implementation are shown below.

```
@ECHO OFF
PATH C:\;C:\DOS;C:\BATCH;C:\UTILS
C:\DOS\APPEND \BATCH
MOUSE
C:\DOS\KEYB UK,,C:\DOS\KEYBOARD.SYS
PROMPT $P$G
SET TEMP=D:\
ECHO HELLO ... This is your PC using
VER
```

As mentioned previously under the COUNTRY section, in PC-DOS 3.3 the extended IBM character set has been changed slightly to accommodate several versions of it by offering several choices on the characters displayed or printed. Each such version is referred to by a specific code page number which is inserted between the two commas of the KEYB UK command and defines the character set to be used. If you intend to use any other code page than 437 (which is the code page for pre-DOS 3.3 versions), then you should refer to your DOS reference guide.

Similarly, some of the possible contents of AUTOEXEC.BAT in a DOS 5 or 6 implementation, are shown below. In the case of DOS 6, REM out (or delete) the second line of the file (SET COMSPEC=); you don't need it.

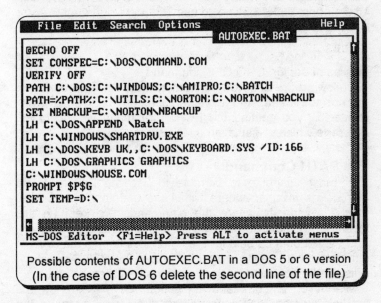

Possible contents of AUTOEXEC.BAT in a DOS 5 or 6 version
(In the case of DOS 6 delete the second line of the file)

Do remember, that any changes made to the AUTOEXEC.BAT file only take effect after typing

AUTOEXEC

at the system prompt, or when re-booting the system by pressing the three keys <Ctrl+Alt+Del> simultaneously, or using the RESET button on your computer.

Below, some of the commands that you can include within the AUTOEXEC.BAT file are explained in some detail, while the rest of the commands are explained briefly in a following list.

The ECHO Command:

If in your AUTOEXEC.BAT file you do not include the command

```
@ECHO OFF
```

you will notice that every time you boot up the system, the commands within your AUTOEXEC.BAT file are echoed (displayed) onto the screen. To avoid such echoes, include the command at the beginning of your AUTOEXEC.BAT file. Users of pre-DOS 3.3 should use

```
ECHO OFF
CLS
```

instead of the @ECHO OFF command.

Following the echo off command, the path, keyboard and prompt commands are executed unseen, until echo is re-activated by executing the ECHO command with a trailing message which is displayed on the screen.

The PATH Command:

It is most desirable to be able to use the DOS external commands from anywhere within the directory tree without having to specify where the commands are kept (in this instance, we have transferred them into the DOS directory). The same could be said for the batch files kept in the BATCH directory, or the utility programs kept in the UTILS directory. This can be achieved by the use of the PATH command.

Whenever a command is issued, DOS searches the current directory and then all the directories listed on the PATH, for the correct file to execute.

PATH can only find program files, that is, executable command files with the extension .EXE or .COM, or files that DOS recognises as containing such commands, as is the case with .BAT files; for data files you must use the APPEND command as is explained on the facing page.

Note the repeated reference to the C: drive within the PATH command, which allows the path to be correctly set even if the user logs onto a drive other than C:.

The APPEND Command:

It is conceivable that the software packages you will be using, require you to type a specific filename in order to activate them. However, some packages also include a second file (most likely a data file which might contain information about the screen display) which is loaded from the first when its name is typed.

In such a case, in addition to including the directory of the package in the PATH command within the AUTOEXEC.BAT file to point to the particular package, you must also include the name of the directory within the APPEND command, otherwise DOS will search for the second (data) file in the root directory, as its extension will most likely be .SCR or .OVL and will not search for it down the PATH.

However, if the second file of a package is an executable file (a file with a .EXE or .COM extension), then you must use the /X switch after its name within the APPEND command.

In the suggested changes to your AUTOEXEC.BAT file, the name of the BATCH directory was included in both the PATH and the APPEND command. This allows you to see the contents of a specific batch file, say those of DOS.BAT (to be discussed in the next chapter), by simply typing at the C:\> prompt:

```
TYPE DOS.BAT
```

If you do not include the BATCH directory in the APPEND command, DOS will not be able to find the file, unless you specify its directory after the TYPE command. Yet when you type at the C:\> prompt:

```
DOS
```

DOS searches down the path, finds the file, recognises it as being a file which contains DOS commands (having the .BAT extension), and executes it.

The APPEND command must be included within the AUTOEXEC.BAT file in a position after the PATH command.

Other commands within the AUTOEXEC.BAT file carry out the following functions:

Command	Function
VERIFY	Turns ON/OFF verification that files are written correctly to disc.
GRAPHICS	Allows DOS to print on a graphics printer the information appearing on the screen. The parameter GRAPHICS indicates that the printer is either an IBM Personal Graphics Printer, an IBM Proprinter, or an IBM Quietwriter printer, while the parameter LASERJETII indicates that the printer is an HP LaserJet II. For other printers see your DOS manual, or look at the Help file (DOS 5 & 6 users only) by typing Help Graphics.
MOUSE	Loads the mouse driver that comes with the mouse device.
KEYB	Identifies the type of keyboard connected to your system.
PROMPT	Changes the appearance of the DOS command prompt. The parameter $P forces the display of the current drive and path, while the parameter $G displays the greater-than sign (>).
SET	Allows an environment variable named TEMP to be associated with the string D:\TEMP. This is the drive and subdirectory where some programs, such as Windows, create and later delete temporary files.
VER	Displays the version of DOS running on your system.

A complete summary of all DOS commands is given in the penultimate chapter of this book.

6. SIMPLE BATCH FILES

To complete the implementation of the hard disc, we need to create a few batch files which we will put in a subdirectory of the root directory, called BATCH. This will help to run the system efficiently. For example, we might require to know the exact name of a DOS command. This can be arranged by creating a batch file for each, to display the corresponding directory whenever the appropriate name is typed. As an example, first create the BATCH subdirectory, using the

```
C:\>MD \BATCH
```

command, then use either **Edit** (or **Edlin**) to create the DOS.BAT file in the BATCH subdirectory, as follows:

```
C:\>edit \BATCH\DOS.BAT
```

and type into the editor's screen the following information:

```
@ECHO OFF
CD \DOS
DIR /P
CD \
```

then save the file using the **File, Save** command (if you are using **Edit**). In line 2, the directory is changed to that of DOS and line 3 causes the contents of the DOS directory to be displayed using the paging (/P) option. Finally, line 4 returns the system back to the root directory.

However, before you can use the DOS.BAT batch file, you must include the subdirectory BATCH within the PATH command of your AUTOEXEC.BAT file. Having done this, save the changes and reboot the system, so that the latest changes to your AUTOEXEC.BAT file can take effect. Now, typing DOS displays the DOS directory, while typing any external MS-DOS command, invokes the appropriate command. A similar batch file can be built for displaying the COMMS directory, the only difference being in line 2 of the file, so that the correct directory is accessed and displayed.

Using Replaceable Parameters

It would be ideal if the language BASIC could be accessed direct from the root directory. However, we can not include the BASIC directory in the PATH command of the AUTOEXEC.BAT file, as we have done with the DOS directory, because there are four main versions of the BASIC language, two of which are included in the IBM PC-DOS system (BASIC and BASICA; A for advanced), GWBASIC (Olivetti's implementation of BASICA) which runs on compatibles, and QBASIC (Microsoft's implementation of an advanced structured BASIC) which has been included with MS-DOS 5 and 6.

Instead, we have to create a rather special batch file in the BATCH subdirectory, using either **Edit** (or **Edlin**), as follows:

```
C:\>edit \BATCH\BAS.BAT
```

and type into the editor's screen the following information:

```
@ECHO OFF
CD \BASIC
%1
CD \
```

Note the variable %1 in the third line which can take the name of any of the four versions of BASIC mentioned above, provided the appropriate variable name is typed after the batch file name. For example, typing

```
BAS QBASIC
```

at the prompt, starts executing the commands within the batch file BAS.BAT, but substituting QBASIC for the %1 variable. Thus, line 3 causes entry into QBASIC, provided it exists in the BASIC directory. Similarly, typing

```
BAS GWBASIC
```

causes entry into GWBASIC, again provided it exists in the BASIC directory. Obviously this batch file design can be applied to other software packages.

As a second example, use your editor to create a new batch file, which we will call ADIR.BAT, as follows:

```
C:\>edit ADIR.BAT
```

and type the following instructions into the editor's screen:

Pre-DOS 6 users

```
@ECHO OFF
DIR \%1 |SORT |MORE
```

DOS 6 users

```
@ECHO OFF
DIR \%1 /P /O:GN
```

The DOS 6 version of this batch file requests a directory listing to be paged (/P), with files displayed in sorted order /O, grouping directories first (G) and listing by name (N) in alphabetical order. This gives a better result, as directories are listed first, not included in the sort, as would be the case with the pre-DOS 6 version.

You can now use this batch file to display the contents of any directory listed in alphabetical order of filename, a page at a time, by simply typing **adir** *directory_name* at the prompt. For *directory_name* you could type **DOS** to have the contents of the **DOS** directory displayed.

Special Batch-file Commands

Apart from all the DOS commands, there are some specific commands which can only be used for batch file processing. These are:

Command	*Action*
CALL	Allows you to call one batch file from within another.
CHOICE	Prompts you to make a choice in a batch file, by pressing one of a specified set of keys, thus allowing you to build menus.

67

ECHO	Enables or disables the screen display of commands executed from within a batch file, or displays the message that follows ECHO.
FOR	Repeats the specified MS-DOS command for each 'variable' in the specified 'set of items'. The general form of the command is:

FOR %%variable IN (set of items) DO command

where command can include any DOS command or a reference to the %%var. For example,

FOR %%X IN (F.OLD F.NEW) DO TYPE %%X

will display F.OLD followed by F.NEW

GOTO label	Transfers control to the line which contains the specified label. For example,

GOTO end

:end

branches to the :end label

IF	Allows conditional command execution. The general form of the command is:

IF [NOT] condition command

where 'condition' can be one of

EXIST filespec
string1==string2
ERRORLEVEL=n

Each of these can be made into a negative condition with the use of the NOT after the IF command.

PAUSE	Suspends execution of the batch file.
REM	Displays comments which follow the REM.
SHIFT	Allows batch files to use more than 10 replaceable parameters. An example of this is as follows:

```
:begin
TYPE %1 | MORE
SHIFT
IF EXIST %1 GOTO begin
REM No more files
```

If we call this batch file SHOW.BAT, then we could look at several different files in succession by simply typing

SHOW file1 file2 file3

as the SHIFT command causes each to be taken in turn.

Combining Batch Files:

After you have created several batch files, one for each application you load onto your hard disc, plus several others to look at file lists in utility subdirectories you will realise that each such batch file takes up 2 or 4KB of disc space, depending on the cluster size of your hard disc, even though individual batch files might only be a few bytes in size. To remedy this situation, you could combine all your batch files into one batch file, call it LOAD.BAT, thus saving considerable disc space.

It will be assumed here that you have 9 batch files which you would like to combine. These might be BATCH.BAT, DOS.BAT, and NORTON.BAT which produce a listing of the corresponding directories, QA.BAT which loads the Q&A integrated package, QPRO.BAT which loads the Quattro spreadsheet, TURBOC.BAT which loads the Turbo C language, SCALC5.BAT, LOTUS24.BAT and LOTUS34.BAT which load the spreadsheets SuperCalc 5, Lotus 1-2-3 Release 2.4 and Lotus 1-2-3 Release 3.4, respectively.

Before we proceed with the writing of the combined batch file, we shall adapt the SHOW.BAT batch file discussed at the end of the previous section, so that we can obtain a listing on the printer of the contents of all the batch files we intend to combine into one, thus making our job easier. The new version of the SHOW.BAT batch file, which should be placed in the BATCH subdirectory, is given below.

```
@ECHO OFF
CD \BATCH
:begin
ECHO %1.bat
@ECHO OFF
TYPE %1.bat |MORE >PRN
SHIFT
IF EXIST %1.bat GOTO begin
ECHO No more files
```

Thus, to obtain a listing of the batch files of interest, simply type

SHOW batch dos norton qa qpro turboc scalc lotus24 lotus34

and press <Enter>. Note that the SHOW batch file has been written in such a way as not to require the extension .BAT to be included after the entry of each of its substitution parameters.

Now, with the help of the listing of these batch files, you can proceed to write the contents of LOAD.BAT, as follows:

```
@ECHO OFF
IF %1==batch GOTO PL1
IF %1==dos GOTO PL2
IF %1==norton GOTO PL3
IF %1==qa GOTO PL4
IF %1==qpro GOTO PL5
IF %1==turboc GOTO PL6
IF %1==scalc GOTO PL7
IF %1==lotus24 GOTO PL8
IF %1==lotus34 GOTO PL9
GOTO END
```

```
:PL1
@echo off
cd\batch
cls
dir/p
GOTO END
:PL2
@echo off
cd\dos
dir/p
GOTO END
:PL3
@echo off
cd\norton
dir/p
GOTO END
:PL4
@echo off
cd\qa
qa
GOTO END
:PL5
@echo off
cd\qpro
q
GOTO END
:PL6
cd\turboc
tc
GOTO END
:PL7
cd\scalc5
sc5
GOTO END
:PL8
@echo off
cd\123r24
lotus
GOTO END
:PL9
@echo off
```

```
cd\123r34
lotus
:END
cd\
```

In the above batch file, we assume that you will be typing the entries corresponding to the substitution parameters in lower case. For example, typing

LOAD qpro

loads the Quattro Pro package.

If you want to make the batch file respond to both uppercase and lower-case letters, then each line containing the IF statement must be repeated, as shown below:

```
IF %1==qpro GOTO PL1
IF %1==QPRO GOTO PL1
```

and so on.

Adopting the lower-case option only, results in a batch file of 596 bytes, which replaces 9 batch files of 301 bytes of total size. However, by doing so you have saved 16 or 32KB of disc space, depending on the cluster size of your disc drive, which is a considerable saving.

The CHOICE Command

With MS-DOS 6, you can streamline your batch files with the adoption of the **choice** command. The general form of this command is:

CHOICE [/C[:]keys] [/N] [/S] [/T[:]c,nn] [text]

where **/C[:]keys** specifies allowable keys in the prompt of the command. For example, if the following command is in a batch file

choice /c:bdn

what you will see on the screen is

[B, D, N]?

Adding text to the command, such as

choice /c:bdn Batch, DOS, or Norton

displays

Batch, DOS, or Norton [B,D,N]?

on the screen.

If you don't use the /C switch, **choice** uses YN (for Yes/No) as the default.

The other command switches have the following meaning:

/N	Causes **choice** not to display the prompt
/S	Causes **choice** to be case sensitive
/T[:]c,nn	Causes **choice** to pause for the specified nn (0-99) seconds, after which it defaults to the specified c character.

As an example, we have rewritten the first part of the LOAD.BAT file, discussed in the previous section, to incorporate the **choice** command, as follows:

```
@ECHO OFF
CLS
ECHO.
ECHO A    Display the BATCH Directory
ECHO B    Display the DOS Directory
ECHO C    Display the NORTON Directory
ECHO.
CHOICE /c:abc Select one -
IF ERRORLEVEL 3 GOTO PL3
IF ERRORLEVEL 2 GOTO PL2
IF ERRORLEVEL 1 GOTO PL1
GOTO END
:PL1
@echo off
cd\batch
cls
dir/p
GOTO END
```

```
:PL2
@echo off
cd\dos
dir/p
GOTO END
:PL3
@echo off
cd\norton
dir/p
GOTO END
:END
cd\
```

Notice that the ERRORLEVEL statements are listed in decreasing order because the statement is true if the parameter returned by **choice** is greater than or equal to the parameter specified in the IF command.

Finally, save this batch file under the filename CHOOSE.BAT.

Stopping Batch File Execution
To stop a batch file before all its statements and commands have been executed, press the two key combination

```
Ctrl+C
```

or

```
Ctrl+Break
```

more than once, if necessary. DOS displays a message asking you if you really want to terminate the batch file. Typing **Y** (for yes), terminates batch file execution.

Ctrl+C and Ctrl+Break Differences:
The main difference between <Ctrl+C> and <Ctrl+Break> is that the former is recognised and acted upon by the resident part of DOS, while the latter is handled by the BIOS. The BIOS also handles directly the <SysReq>, <Ctrl+Alt+Del>, and <Print Screen> commands. However, the <Ctrl+Break> command can only be effective if BREAK has been switched

on from within your CONFIG.SYS file, which can marginally slow down the performance of machines with a less powerful processor than an 80386.

Normally, when you press a key, the BIOS generates a hardware interrupt and leaves it up to DOS to handle it. DOS, in turn, places each keystroke or command (which it interprets as characters) into a queue and passes each one to the appropriate program or the COMMAND processor.

Thus, pressing <Ctrl+C> causes the BIOS to pass the command to DOS to be dealt with when DOS is able to do so, whether BREAK is on or not. However, for <Ctrl+C> to work, it must be the first, or only, command left in the buffer. In addition, the hardware interrupts must not have been switched off by the running program, otherwise DOS would not have been aware that the command had been issued. To overcome this, press <Ctrl+C> a few times in rapid succession to ensure that DOS is listening and that it is the first one in the buffer.

* * *

If you would like to be able to write customised batch files, create specialist programs with the use of the DEBUG program and learn how to design your own professional looking menu screens, then may we suggest that you refer to either the book entitled *A Concise Advanced User's Guide to MS-DOS* (BP264), or the book entitled *Making MS-DOS Work For You* (BP319) also published by Bernard Babani (publishing) Ltd.

* * *

7. MANAGING YOUR SYSTEM

MS-DOS provides several commands which help you to manage and control your system's environment. Some of these commands are internal MS-DOS commands and some are external. First we discuss the internal commands.

Changing the Access Date of a File

If your computer is not fitted with a battery backed clock and you have not been entering the correct time and date on booting up the system, then all your saved files will be showing the default date 1/1/80 in the directory entry. To change this date for a given file, set the current TIME and DATE and type

```
C:\>COPY filespec + filespec
```

where filespec stands for drive, path, filename and extension. Ignore the message 'Content of destination file lost before copy' given by MS-DOS when this command has been executed.

The SET Command

To find out what parameters have been set up, type

```
C:\>SET
```

at the prompt which would evoke the response

```
COMSPEC=C:\COMMAND.COM
PATH=C:\;C:DOS;C:\COMMS
PROMPT=$P$G
```

COMSPEC shows which Command Processor is being used by the system, while PATH and PROMPT display the corresponding commands in your AUTOEXEC.BAT file.

The TYPE Command

This command allows you to see on screen the contents of text files. The command takes the form:

```
C:\>TYPE filespec
```

This command is useful because it only lets you have a look at the contents of files without changing the environment in any way.

For example, if you ever wanted to find out what is held in either the CONFIG.SYS or AUTOEXEC.BAT files, then use this command rather than the editor.

If the text file you are looking at is longer than one screen full, then use <Ctrl+S> key sequence (while holding down the key marked **Ctrl**, press the **S** key once) to stop the scrolling of the display. Any key will start the display scrolling again.

Using TYPE on other than ASCII files (such as a .COM or .EXE file) could cause your system to 'hang' as a result of attempting to display certain sequence of machine code that might be contained in the file. If that happens, use the <Ctrl+Alt+Del> key sequence to re-boot the system.

In general, to use the TYPE command to see the contents of files, you must be logged into the subdirectory where the file is found or give the full filespec. For example, to look at the contents of the DOS.BAT file (which is to be found in the BATCH subdirectory) when at the C:\> prompt, you will have to use:

```
C:\>TYPE \BATCH\DOS.BAT
```

Alternatively, if you include the BATCH subdirectory in an APPEND command following the PATH command within the AUTOEXEC.BAT file, then you could omit the subdirectory in the TYPE command. Thus, the BATCH subdirectory must be included in the PATH command to be able to find and execute the various batch files, but in order to find any of these files from within a DOS command, such as TYPE, the subdirectory must also be included in the APPEND command.

The TYPE command could be used to direct text files to the printer by typing

```
C:\>TYPE EXAMPLE.TXT >PRN
```

where PRN stands for 'printer' which is connected to the parallel printer port.

The VER & VOL Commands

To find out which version of MS-DOS/PC-DOS you are currently using, type

```
C:\>VER
```

at the prompt.
   To find out the volume label of the disc in the logged drive, type

```
C:\>VOL
```

at the prompt. If the disc was not labelled during formatting, then the computer will respond with

```
Volume in drive B has no label
```

otherwise the appropriate label will be displayed.

The PRINT & PRTSC Commands

The first time the PRINT command is used it has to be loaded into memory as it is an external MS-DOS command. However, from then on It resides in memory and can be used without having to re-load it.
   The PRINT command provides background printing, that is, it can print long files while you are doing something else with your computer. In fact, using this command provides you with a print spooler which allows you to make and control a queue of several files for printing. The command takes the form:

```
C:\>PRINT filespec        adds filespec to print queue
```

```
C:\>PRINT filespec /C     cancels printing that file
C:\>PRINT /T              terminates all printing
C:\>PRINT                 displays files in queue
```

The PRINT command assumes that you have continuous paper in your printer. There is no facility to pause printing.

To print the two text files TEXT1.DOC and TEXT2.DOC, type

```
C:\>PRINT TEXT1.DOC
C:\>PRINT TEXT2.DOC
```

Wildcard characters can also be used in the command, as follows:

```
C:\>PRINT TEXT*.DOC
```

which will spool all the files starting with the characters TEXT and having the extension .DOC to the printer.

Text which is displayed on the screen can be sent to the printer by pressing the Print Screen (<Shift+PrtSc>) key.

On the other hand, pressing the <Ctrl> and <Print_Screen> keys simultaneously causes re-direction of output to the printer. To cancel the effect, repeat the same key stroke.

Backing-up and Restoring Hard Discs

The pre-DOS 6 BACKUP command and the DOS 6 MSBACKUP utility allow you to archive important files from your hard disc and generate back-up copies on floppy discs.

The BACKUP Command - Pre-DOS 6 Users:

The external BACKUP command takes the form:

BACKUP *source destination options*

where **source** is the drive/path/files to be backed up,
      destination is the drive to back-up to, and
      options are:

80

/A   to add the files to a disc in the destination
          drive

/D:*date* to back-up only files from the specified date
          onwards

/M   to back-up only files modified since they
          were last backed up

/S   to also back-up sub-directories of the source
          path.

Thus, to back-up, for the first time, all the word processor files
whose path is \DATABASE\WPFILES, type

    `C:\>BACKUP C:\DATABASE\WPFILES\*.* A:`

while to back-up only files modified since they were last
backed up, type

    `C:\>BACKUP C:\DATABASE\WPFILES\*.* A:/M`

In both cases, the wildcard characters *.* ensures that all files
with all their extensions in the WPFILES subdirectory are
backed up.

The RESTORE external command allows you to
de-archive files. It is the only utility which can restore to the
hard disc files previously copied to floppy discs using the
BACKUP utility. The command takes the form:

    RESTORE *source destination options*

where **source** is the drive to restore from,
        destination is the drive/path/files to restore, and
        options are:

        /P to prompt Y/N? before restoring, and
        /S to also restore files from sub-directories.

Thus, typing

    `C:\>RESTORE A: C:\DATABASE\WPFILES\*.*/P`

restores selected files from the floppy disc in the A: drive to
the subdirectory WPFILES in the C: drive, provided these
files were backed up from the same named subdirectories.

81

The MSBACKUP Utility - DOS 6 Users:

The MSBACKUP utility comes in two versions, one for DOS and one for Windows. A graphical front-end controls all the functions once the program is started.

By default backed up files are compressed at a ratio which depends on the type of files being handled. In our experience word processor files with embedded graphics can compress at up to an 8:1 ratio, while binary files can compress to around 1.4:1. We have managed to backup a 17 Mbyte subdirectory onto only two 1.44 Mbyte floppy discs and in only a few minutes as well!

Configuring Your System

Before using MSBACKUP carry out the following two steps. At the DOS prompt type

```
MD C:\BACKUP
```

then enter the line below into the AUTOEXEC.BAT file

```
SET MSDOSDATA=C:\BACKUP
```

This sets a DOS environmental variable which will tell the MSBACKUP program where to find its configuration files, each time it starts up. Restart your computer to make the instruction immediately effective.

The first time you run MSBACKUP you get an 'Alert' message saying that Backup needs configuration. Press <Enter> to start the process, which only takes about five minutes. Accept all the video and mouse defaults, unless of course your system is non standard, in which case you will certainly know about it by now.

Your floppy and hard disc drives are tested and configured next, as is your main processor. You are then faced with the Configure dialogue box, from within which you should run the **Compatibility Test**, which carries out a small trial Backup and Compare operation to test the system. You will need two similar and numbered floppy discs.

To start an actual backup and restore procedure type

```
C:\>MSBACKUP
```

Next, select **Backup** from the opening dialogue box. This opens a further dialogue box from which you set all the backup options, select files to backup (by clicking them with the right mouse button - it might be necessary to **Exclude** all files and subdirectories, before using **Include** to make your selection), and choose the destination for the backup, which should be your A: floppy drive. Finally, check the estimated number of disks and space required and make sure you have that number of labelled disks ready, then click the **Start Backup** button to begin making the backup. If this button is greyed out, it means that no files have been selected for back up.

As part of the backup process, MSBACKUP creates a backup catalogue that contains information about the files you backed up and places one copy on your hard disk, and another copy on the disk or network drive that contains your backup set. When you need to restore any of the files, you need to load the backup catalogue set. Each catalogue set is given a unique name that helps you identify a backup set.

To restore your files and directory structure start MSBACKUP, and select **Restore** from the opening dialogue box. If the restoring is being carried out on a hard disc from which the backup was taken, then a catalogue will exist on the hard drive and will be loaded automatically.

If the original backup was carried out on another computer, or you have more than one catalogue set and you don't remember which is which, then you will need to copy it from the last floppy disc of the backup set by pressing the **Catalog** button and using first the **Retrieve** option to retrieve the required catalogue, then the **Load** option. Finally, right-click the **[-C-]** item in the **Restore Files** list to change it to **[-C-] All Files**, and press the **Start Restore** button.

The DOSKEY Utility

MS-DOS 5 and 6 comes with an external utility called DOSKEY. This utility, when loaded into your system, allows you to recall the most recently entered DOS commands at the system prompt, for subsequent use, which can save you a lot of retyping. You will find that learning to use DOSKEY will be extremely useful to you.

DOSKEY is an example of a special type of program, called TSR (terminate-and-stay-resident). Once a TSR is loaded into memory, it stays in the background without interfering with the other programs you are running. To load DOSKEY into RAM, type

```
DOSKEY
```

at the system prompt and press <Enter>. This causes a message to appear on your screen informing you that the program has been loaded into memory.

If you are going to use DOSKEY frequently, it will be better to include the line

```
C:\DOS\DOSKEY
```

in your AUTOEXEC.BAT file, which loads the program automatically every time you switch on your system.

If you have a computer with an 80386 or higher processor, you should load DOSKEY in the upper memory with the command

```
LH C:\DOS\DOSKEY
```

so as to avoid occupying about 3 Kbytes of conventional memory.

Once DOSKEY is in memory, every time you type a command at the system prompt, the command is stored in the DOSKEY buffer which is 512 bytes long. To illustrate how this works, type the following commands, pressing <Enter> at the end of each line:

```
TYPE CONFIG.SYS
```

and after the contents of the CONFIG.SYS file have been displayed on screen, type

```
TYPE AUTOEXEC.BAT
```

and after the contents of the AUTOEXEC.BAT file have been displayed, type the commands

```
COPY CONFIG.SYS \BATCH
COPY AUTOEXEC.BAT \BATCH
```

The last two commands copy the two precious files into the \BATCH subdirectory, for safety's sake.

To recall the most recently executed DOS command, simply press the <↑> key. Each time this is pressed, the next most recently executed DOS command is displayed. In our case, pressing the <↑> key 4 times, takes us to the first command typed in the above example.

When the required command is displayed at the prompt, pressing the <←> or <→> keys allows you to edit the recalled command, while pressing <Enter> re-executes the chosen command.

The key movements associated with DOSKEY, are as follows:

Key	Result
↑	Displays the previous command in the buffer list.
↓	Displays the next command in the buffer list.
F7	Displays a numbered list of the commands in the buffer.
F8	Cycles through the commands in the buffer that start with a letter you specify.
F9	Prompts you for the number of the stored command in the list (obtained by using the F7 function key).
PgUp	Displays the first command in the buffer list.
PgDn	Displays the last command in the buffer list.
Esc	Clears the command at the prompt.
Alt+F7	Clears the list of commands from the buffer.

* * *

MS-DOS has many more commands which can be used to control a micro in special ways. However, this is an area which lies outside the scope of this book. What was covered here, together with the summary of the DOS commands given in the penultimate section of this book, is more than enough to allow effective control of a microcomputer.

* * *

8. COMMAND SUMMARY

The following is a list of all the commands supported by the MS-DOS operating environment. The various commands are labelled internal or external, with external commands being accessible to the user only if the full filespec (drive and path) is given to where the appropriate command file resides. Examples of command usage are given whenever possible.

DOS 6 does not support the ASSIGN.COM, EXEC2BIN.EXE, GRAFTABL.COM, and JOIN.EXE command files. These together with 4201.CPI, 4208.CPI, 5202.CPI, LINK.EXE, MSHERC.COM, PRINTER.SYS, and SMARTDRV.SYS, which are left behind in your DOS subdirectory when you upgrade from a previous version of DOS, can safely be deleted to free some 164 Kbytes of disc space.

Command	Explanation
append	External - sets a path that MS-DOS will search for data files when they are not in the current directory. It can even be told not to search already defined paths.

Example: append c:\wproc\docs

searches the \wproc\docs directory on drive c: for data files.

Switches:
/e   assigns the list of appended directories to an environment variable named APPEND. This switch can be used only the first time you use APPEND after starting your system. If you use /E, you can use the SET command to display the list of appended directories.

/path:on   specifies whether a program is to search appended directories for a data file when a path is already Included with the name of the file the program is looking for.

/path:off specifies that a program is not to search appended directories. The default is /path:on.

/x:on   Specifies whether DOS is to search appended directories when executing programs. You can abbreviate /x:on to /x. If you want to specify x:on, do it the first time you use APPEND after starting your system.

/x:off Specifies whether DOS is not to search appended directories when executing programs. The default value is /x:off.

attrib [filespec]   External - sets or resets the *read only* attribute & archive bit of a file, and displays the attributes of a file.

Switches:
+a sets the archive bit of a file.
−a clears the archive bit.
+h sets the file as a hidden file.
−h clears the hidden file attribute.
+r sets read-only mode of a file.
−r disables read-only mode.
+s sets the file as a system file.
−s clears the system file attribute.
/s processes files in the current directory and its subdirectories.

Example: attrib +r filespec

break

Internal - sets the <Ctrl+Break> or the extended <Ctrl+C> checking. This command can be used either at the command prompt or in the CONFIG.SYS file.

Example: break ON

buffers

Internal - allocates memory for a specified number of disc buffers (1-99) from within your CONFIG.SYS file.

Example: buffers=40,m

where m is optional and specifies the number of the secondary buffer cache (0-8).

call

Internal - calls one batch file from another without exiting from the first one.

cd (or chdir)

Internal - changes the working directory to a different directory.

Example: cd\wproc\docs

chcp [nnn]

Internal - selects current code page for as many devices as possible. Omitting *nnn* displays the current code page.

chkdsk [filespec]

External - has been replaced by SCANDISK in DOS 6.2. CHKDSK analyses the directories, files, and File Allocation Table (FAT) on the logged or designated drive and produces a status report. It also reports the volume, serial number and disc allocation units.

Switches:

/f fixes any problems found during the check.

/v causes the display of filespecs as they are being processed.

Example: chkdsk a:/f/v

choice
External - prompts the user to make a choice in a batch file.

Switches:

/c:keys specifies allowable keys in the prompt. When displayed, the keys will be followed by a question mark. If you don't specify the /c switch, choice uses YN as the default.

/n causes choice not to display the prompt. The text before the prompt is still displayed, however. If you specify the /n switch, the specified keys are still valid.

/s causes choice to be case sensitive.

/t:c,nn causes choice to pause for a specified number of seconds nn (0-99), before defaulting to a specified key, shown above as switch c.

cls
Internal - clears the screen.

command [filespec]
External - starts the command processor which is loaded into memory in two parts; the resident part and the transient part.

If the transient part is overwritten by a program, it is reloaded.

Switches:
/c executes a following command.
/e specifies the environment size in bytes (160-32768, default = 160 bytes).
/k runs the specified program or batch file and then displays the DOS command prompt.
/p prohibits command.com from exiting to a higher level.

Example:
command /c chkdsk a:

starts a new command processor under the current program, runs the chkdsk command on the disc in the A: drive, and returns to the first command processor.

copy [filespec]

Internal - copies one or more files to specified disc. If preferred, copies can be given different names.

Switches:
/a indicates an ASCII text file.
/b indicates a binary file.
/v causes the verification of data written on the destination disc.

Example: copy *.exe a:/v

copies all files with the .exe extension to the a: drive with verification.

country

External - enables DOS to use country-specific conventions for displaying dates, times, and currency. Used only in CONFIG.SYS.

ctty	Internal - changes the standard I/O console to an auxiliary (aux) console, and vice versa.
	Example: ctty aux
	moves all input/output from the current device (console) to an aux port such as another terminal.
	The command *ctty con* moves I/O back to the console.
	Valid values for the device parameter are prn, lpt1, lpt2, lpt3, con, aux, com1, com2, com3, and com4.
date	Internal - enters or changes the current date.
dblspace	External - starts the DoubleSpace program to set-up or configure compressed drives. Don't use this command from within Windows.
debug	External - starts the debug program that allows you to create or edit executable files.
defrag	External - reorganises files on a disc to optimise performance. Do not use this command from within Windows. Use the command by itself to open up a front-end, or with the following switches.
	Switches:
	/b restarts your computer after files have been reorganised.

/bw	starts program using a black and white colour system.
/f	defragments files and ensures that the disk contains no empty spaces between files.
/g0	disables the graphic mouse and graphic character set.
/h	moves hidden files.
/lcd	starts program using an lcd colour system.
/u	defragments files and leaves empty spaces, if any, between files.
/skiphigh	loads program into conventional memory. By default, it is loaded into upper memory, if available.
/s	controls how the files are sorted in their directories. If you omit this switch, it uses the current order on the disk. The following list describes each of the values you can use to sort files. Use any combination of the values, and do not separate these values with spaces.
d	by date and time, earliest first.
d–	by date and time, latest first.
e	in alphabetic order by extension.

<table>
<tr><td></td><td>e–</td><td>in reverse alphabetic order by extension.</td></tr>
<tr><td></td><td>n</td><td>in alphabetic order by name.</td></tr>
<tr><td></td><td>n–</td><td>in reverse alphabetic order by name.</td></tr>
<tr><td></td><td>s</td><td>by size, smallest first.</td></tr>
<tr><td></td><td>s–</td><td>by size, largest first.</td></tr>
</table>

del [filespec]

Internal - deletes all files with the designated filespec.

Switch:
/p displays filenames to confirm deletion.

Example: del a:*.txt
deletes all .txt files from the a: drive.

deltree

External - deletes a specified directory and all the files and sub-directories that might be in it.

Switch:
/y carries out the command without first prompting you for confirmation.

device

Internal - loads a specified device driver into memory from within your CONFIG.SYS file.

devicehigh

External - loads a specified device driver into upper memory from within your CONFIG.SYS file.

dir [filespec]

Internal - lists the files in a directory.

Switches:
/a displays only the names of those directories and files with the attributes you specify.

For example,

a backup files.
−a files not changed since last backup.
d directory.
−d files only (not directories).
h hidden files.
−h not hidden files.
r read-only files.
−r files other than read-only.
s system files.
−s non-system files.

/b lists each directory name or file, one per line (including the file extension).

/c displays information about file-compression ratios on Double Space drives.

/l displays unsorted directory and filenames in lower case.

/o: controls the sort order in which a directory listing is displayed. For example,

c by compression ratio (lowest first).
−c by compression ratio (highest first).
d by date & time, earliest first.
−d by date & time, latest first.
e in alphabetical order by extension.
−e in reverse alphabetical order by extension.
g with directories grouped before files.
−g with directories grouped after files.
n in alphabetical order.

	–n in reverse alphabetical order.
	s by size, smallest first.
	–s by size, largest first.

/p displays the directory listing a page at a time.

/s lists every occurrence, in the specified directory and all sub directories, of the specified filename.

/w displays the directory listing in wide format.

diskcomp   External - compares the contents of the disc in the source drive to the disc in the destination drive.

diskcopy   External - copies the contents of the disc in the source drive to the disc in the destination drive.

Switches:

/v verifies correct copying.

/m forces multi-pass copy using memory only.

dos   Internal - specifies that DOS should maintain a link to the upper memory area, load part of itself into high memory area (HMA), or both. This command can only be used from within your CONFIG.SYS file.

doskey   External - starts the doskey pro-gram which recalls DOS commands.

Switches:

/bufsize= allows the specification of the buffer size to be

	used for storing commands. The default size is 512 bytes, while the minimum buffer size is 256 bytes.
/insert	switches on the 'insert' mode.
/history	displays a list of all commands stored in memory. The switch can be used with the re-direction symbol (>) to redirect the list to a file.
/macros	displays a list of all doskey macros. The switch can be used with the re-direction symbol (>) to redirect the list to a file.
/overstrike	switches on the 'overstrike' mode.
/reinstall	installs a new copy of doskey and clears the buffer of the current copy.

dosshell
External - activates the front-end graphical interface (not distributed with version 6.2).

drivparm
External - allows you to define parameters for devices such as disc and tape drives when you start your computer. This command can only be used from within your CONFIG.SYS file.

echo
Internal - sets ECHO to on or off.

edit	External - activates the MS-DOS screen editor which is used to create or edit ASCII text files.

Switches:
/b displays the editor in black and white.
/g uses the fastest screen updating for CGA displays.
/h displays the maximum number of lines possible for the monitor you are using.

emm386	External - enables or disables expanded memory support on a computer with an 80386 or higher processor.

erase	Internal - see del command.

exit	Internal - exits the command processor and returns to a previous level.

expand	External - expands a compressed file from a system disc.

fasthelp	External - provides a short summary of DOS 6 commands.

fastopen [filespec]	External - store in memory the location of directories and recently opened files on a specified drive.

Switch:
/x allows use of expanded memory. If this switch is used, then the /x switch must also be used with the BUFFERS command.

fc [filespec]

External - compares two files and displays the differences between them.

Switches:

/a abbreviates the output of an ASCII comparison to only the first and last line of each set of differences.

/b compares binary files.

/c ignores the case of letters.

/l compares ASCII files line by line.

/n displays the line numbers during an ASCII comparison.

/t does not expand tabs to spaces.

/w compresses tabs and spaces during the comparison.

fcbs

Internal - specifies the number of file control blocks (FCBs) that DOS can have open at the same time (1-255, default = 4). This command can only be used from within your CONFIG.SYS file.

fdisk

External - sets up and partitions the fixed disc for use with DOS and other operating systems. It is also used to display and change the current active partition. The command supports an 80-column screen. It also has improved user-friendly commands to allow disc partitioning in megabytes or percentages instead of cylinders.

Switch:

/status displays an overview of the partition information without starting FDISK.

files	Internal - specifies the number of files that DOS can access at one time. This command can only be used from within your CONFIG.SYS file.
find [filespec]	External - searches for a specific string of text in a specified ASCII file or files.

Switches:

/c prints the count of lines containing the string.

/i search is insensitive to the case of letters.

/n precedes each occurrence with the relative line number in the file.

/v displays all lines not containing the specified string.

Example: find "lost words" chap1 searches for the string *lost words* (which must appear within full quotes) in the named file (chap1).

for	Internal - repeats a command for each item in a set. This command can only be used at the command prompt or from within a batch file.
format [filespec]	External - formats the disc in the specified drive.

Switches:

/4 formats a double-sided disc with 40 tracks, 9 sectors per track for 360 Kbytes in a high capacity (1.2 Mbytes) disc drive per track.

/8 formats with 8 sectors per track.

/b reserves space for the system files.

/f:*size*

specifies the size of the disc to be formatted. Use one of the following values for size, which specifies the capacity of the disc in Kbytes:

160 / 180 for single-sided, double-density 5¼" discs,
320 / 360 for double-sided, double-density 5¼" discs,
720 for double-sided, double-density 3½" discs,
1200 for double-sided, high-capacity 5¼" discs,
1440 for double-sided, high-capacity 3½" discs,
2880 for 2.88 Mbytes, double-sided, 3½" discs.

/n specifies the number of sectors per track, i.e. /n:9 for nine sectors.

/q deletes the file allocation table (FAT) and the root directory of a previously formatted disc.

/s copies the system files from the logged drive.

/t specifies the number of tracks, i.e. /t:40 for forty tracks.

/v:label

allows you to specify *label* without prompting after the formatting process.

Example: format a:/4/s

goto

Internal - jumps to a labelled line within the same batch file.

graphics	External - it supports EGA and VGA graphics modes to provide screen dumps to IBM Graphics, Proprinters and compatibles.

Switches:

/b   prints the background in colour.

/lcd prints an image by using the liquid crystal display aspect ratio instead of the CGA aspect ratio.

/r   prints the image as it appears on the screen (white characters on a black background, rather than reversed).

help   External - provides online information about the DOS commands.

Switches:

/b   allows use of monochrome monitor with a colour graphics card.

/g   provides fast update of a CGA screen.

/h   displays maximum number of lines possible with your hardware.

/nohi allows use of monitor that does not support high intensity.

if   Allows conditional execution of commands within a batch file.

include   Internal - includes the contents of one configuration block within another. This command can only be used from within your CONFIG.SYS file.

install	Internal - loads a memory-resident program into memory. This command can only be used from within your CONFIG.SYS file.
interlnk	External - starts the INTERLNK program, which connects two computers via their parallel or serial ports and enables them to share discs and printer ports.
intersvr	External - starts the INTERLNK server.
keyb [xx]	External - selects a special keyboard layout. Omitting **xx** returns the current status of the keyboard.
	Switches: /e specifies that an enhanced keyboard is installed. /id: specifies the keyboard in use.
label	External - creates or changes the volume identification label on a disc.
lastdrive	Internal - specifies the maximum number of drives you can access. This command can only be used from within your CONFIG.SYS file.
loadfix	External - forces programs to load above the first 64 Kbytes of conventional memory.
loadhigh (lh)	Internal - loads a program into the upper memory area.
md (or mkdir)	Internal - creates a new directory on the specified disc.

mem   External - it reports the amounts of
                       conventional, expanded and ex-
                       tended memory that are available.

                       Switches:
                       /c   displays the status of
                                 programs loaded in con-
                                 ventional and upper
                                 memory area.
                       /d   displays the status of
                                 currently loaded pro-
                                 grams and of internal
                                 drivers.
                       /free   lists the free areas of
                                 conventional and upper
                                 memory.
                       /module   shows how a program
                                 module is currently using
                                 memory.
                       /page   pages screen output.
                                 Can be used with all the
                                 other switches.

memmaker   External - starts the MemMaker
                       program, which optimises your
                       computer's memory by configuring
                       device drivers and memory
                       resident programs to run in the
                       upper memory area. Don't use this
                       program from within Windows.

                       Switches:
                       /b   displays MemMaker
                                 in black and white.
                       /batch   forces it to take all the
                                 default options.
                       /session used by MemMaker
                                 during memory
                                 optimisation.
                       /swap:drive specifies the letter of
                                 the original start-up
                                 drive.

/t	disables the detection of Token Ring networks.
/undo	forces MemMaker to undo the most recent changes.
/w:s1,s2	specifies the amount of upper memory space for Windows translation buffers.

menucolor   External - sets the text and back-ground colours for the start-up menu. This command can only be used from within a menu block in your CONFIG.SYS file.

menudefault   External - specifies the default menu item on the start-up menu and sets a time-out value, if desired. This command can only be used from within a menu block in your CONFIG.SYS file.

menuitem   External - defines up to nine items on the start-up menu. This com-mand can only be used from within a menu block in your CONFIG.SYS file.

mode [options] External - sets the mode of opera-tion on a display monitor, parallel/serial printer or the RS232C port. The keyboard repe-tition and auto-repeat start delay time can be set. Also, it allows the setting of the number of rows to any of 25, 43 or 50 on the screen, and there is a wider range of serial-port configurations.

Options:

Display: mode [n]

40	sets display width to 40 characters per line.
80	sets display width to 80 characters per line.
bw40	sets screen to black and white display with 40 characters.
bw80	sets screen to black and white display with 80 characters.
co40	sets screen to colour display with 40 characters.
co80	sets screen to colour display with 80 characters.
mono	sets screen to monochrome with 80 characters.

Printer: mode LPTi: [n][,[m][,p]]

i	sets printer number with legal values from 1 to 3.
n	sets number of characters per line with legal values of 80 or 132.
m	sets the number of lines per inch with legal values of 6 or 8.
p	allows continuous re-entry on a time-out error.

Example: mode LPT1: 132,8

sets the printer in the first parallel port to 132 characters per line and 8 lines per inch.

Serial printer: mode LPTi:=COMj
It redirects all output sent to one of the parallel printer ports to one of the serial (RS232C) ports.

106

Before using this command, the serial port must be initialised using the *p* switch of the printer mode command.

i   sets printer number with legal values from 1 to 3.

j   sets the serial port with legal values of 1 or 2.

more   External - sends output to the console one screen-full at a time.

Example: type read.me | more

displays the contents of the read.me file one screen at a time.

move   External - moves one or more files to the specified location. It can also be used to rename files and directories.

msav   External - starts the Anti-Virus program, which scans your computer for known viruses.

Switches:

/a scans all drives except drive A: and B:.

/c scans and removes viruses from specified drive.

/l scans all local drives except network drives.

/n lists contents of MSAV file.

/r reports and lists files checked in MSAV file.

/s scans specified drive but does not remove viruses.

Several other switches exist which control your hardware. To find out more about these, use Help.

msbackup	External - starts the BACKUP program, which backs up or restores one or more files from one disc onto another.
mscdex	External - provides access to CD-ROM drives.
msd	External - starts the Diagnostics program, which provides technical information on your computer.
nlsfunc	External - provides support for extended country information and allows the use of CHCP command to select code pages for all devices defined as having code page switching support.
numlock	Internal - specifies whether the NUMLOCK key is set ON or OFF. This command can only be used from within your CONFIG.SYS file.
path	Internal - sets and displays the path to be searched by DOS for external commands or batch files.
	Example: path c:\;c:\dos;c:\comms
	will search the root directory as well as the DOS and COMMS sub-directories for files with .COM, .EXE, and .BAT extensions.
pause	Internal - suspends processing of a batch file and displays a message that prompts you to press any key to continue.
power	External - turns power management on or off, reports the status

of power management, and sets levels of power conservation.

print [filespec]　　External - can be used to print text files in background mode, while other tasks are being performed. Using the command without options displays files already in the print queue.

Switches:
/b　sets size of internal buffer with legal values from 512 to 16384 bytes, speeding up printing.
/c　allows cancellation of files in the print queue. It can be used with the /p switch.
/d　specifies the print device such as PRN or AUX.
/p　allows the addition of files to the print queue. Both /c & /p can be used in the same command line.
/q　specifies the number of files in the print queue, normally 10, with legal values from 4 to 32.
/t　allows cancellation of files in the print queue.

prompt　　Internal - changes the command prompt.

Example: pg

which allows the path of the current working directory to be displayed as the prompt.

qbasic　　External - activates the MS-DOS QBasic program that reads instructions written in the Basic computer language.

Switches:

/b	displays QBasic in black and white.
/editor	activates the MS-DOS screen editor.
/g	provides the fastest update of a CGA monitor.
/h	displays the maximum number of display lines possible for the type of monitor used.
/nohi	allows use of a monitor that does not support high intensity.
/run	runs the specified Basic program before displaying it.

rd (or rmdir)	Internal - removes the specified directory.
rem	Enables you to include comments in batch files.
ren (or rename)	Internal - changes the file name.

Example: ren a:\doc\mem1 mem2

will rename the mem1 file, which is to be found in subdirectory doc on a disc in the a: drive, to mem2.

replace [options]	External - allows easy updating of files from a source disc to a target disc of files having the same name.

Switches:

/a adds new files that exist on the source disc but not on the target disc. This switch can not be used with the /s or /u switch.

/p prompts the user before replacing.

/r replaces read only files, as well as unprotected files.

/s searches all subdirectories of the destination directory and replaces matching files. You can not use the /s switch with the /a switch.

/u updates files with a time and date on the source disc more recent than those on the destination disc. You can not use the /u switch with the /a switch.

/w waits for you to insert a disc before replace begins to search for source files.

restore [options]

External - restores one or more files that were backed up using the *backup* command of DOS versions 2.0 - 5.0. This command is NOT used for DOS version 6 backup files.

Switches:

/a:date or /b:date

restores those files last modified on or before the specified date. The date format varies according to the country setting in your CONFIG.SYS file.

/d displays a list of the files on the backup disc that match the names specified in *filename* without restoring any files.

/e:time or /l:time

restores only those files last modified on or before the specified time (according to the country setting).

/m restores only those files modified since the last backup.

/n restores only those files that no longer exist on the destination disc.

/p prompts user before overwriting an existing file by restoring.

/s restores files in the specified directory and all files in any sub-directories of the specified directory.

scandisk

External - scans and repairs specified discs.

Switches:

/all checks and repairs all local drives.

/autofix fixes damage without prompting you first. By default, if you start Scan-Disk with this switch and it finds lost clusters on your drive, it saves the lost clusters as files in the drive's root directory.

/checkonly

checks a drive for errors, but does not repair any damage. You cannot use this switch with the /auto-fix or /custom switches.

/custom runs ScanDisk using the configuration settings in the [Custom] section of the SCANDISK.INI file. The switch is useful for running ScanDisk from a batch program. It can't be used with the /autofix or /checkonly switches.

/mono	configures ScanDisk to use a monochrome display. Instead of specifying this switch every time you run ScanDisk, include the 'display=mono' line in your SCANDISK.INI file.
/nosave	directs ScanDisk to delete any lost clusters it finds. Can be used only with the /autofix switch.
/nosummary	
	prevents ScanDisk from displaying a full-screen summary after checking each drive.
/surface	automatically performs a surface scan after checking other areas of a drive. During a surface scan of an uncompressed drive, it confirms that data can be reliably written and read from the scanned drive. During a surface scan of a DoubleSpace drive, it confirms that data can be decompressed.

set

Internal - sets strings into the command processor's environment. The general form of the command is:

set [name=[parameter]]

Set by itself displays the current environment.

setver

External - displays the version table.

share	External - installs file sharing and locking.

Switches:
/f: allocates file space, in bytes. The default value is 2048.
/l: sets the number of files that can be locked at one time. The default is 20.

shell	Internal - specifies the name and location of the command interpreter you want DOS to use. This command can only be used from within your CONFIG.SYS file.

shift	Internal - allows more than 10 replaceable parameters in a batch file.

smartdrv	External - creates a disc cache in extended memory which speeds up access to your hard disc. This command can either be used at the command prompt or from within your AUTOEXEC.BAT file.

Parameters:
[[drive+|-]   Specifies the letter of the drive for caching control. The plus (+) sign enables caching, while the minus (−) sign disables it. A drive letter without a plus or minus sign, enables read-caching and disables write-caching.

Switches:
/e:size   specifies in bytes the 'element' size of the cache that moves at a time. Valid values are 1024, 2048, 4096, and 8192

(default=8192). The larger the size, the more conventional memory is used.

/b:size   specifies the 'buffer' size in kilobytes of the read-ahead buffer - the additional data read from the hard disc by an application (default=16K)

/c   writes all cached data from memory to disc - use this option if you are going to turn off your computer.

/r   clears the contents of the existing cache and restarts SMARTDrive.

/l   prevents SMARTDrive from automatically loading into upper memory blocks, even if these are available. You can use this switch if upper memory is enabled for use by programs.

/q   stops status messages when SMARTDrive starts. This switch cannot be used with the /v switch.

/v   enables SMARTDrive to display status and error messages when it starts. (By default, it does not display any messages unless it encounters an error condition.) This switch cannot be used with the /q switch.

/s   displays extra information about SMARTDrive's status.

sort [filespec]	External - reads data from the console or a file, sorts it and sends it to the console or file.
	Switches:
	/r sorts in reverse order.
	/+n sorts the file according to the character in column n.
	Example: dir | sort
	sorts the output of the *dir* command in alphabetical order.
stacks	Internal - supports the dynamic use of data stacks to handle hardware interrupts. Use only from within the CONFIG.SYS file.
submenu	Internal - defines an item on a start-up menu that, when selected, displays another set of options. Use only from within the CONFIG.SYS file.
subst	External - allows substitution of a virtual drive for an existing drive and path.
	Switch:
	/d deletes a virtual drive.
	Example: subst d: a:\wproc\docs
	will cause future reference to drive d: to be taken as replacement to the longer reference to a:\wproc\docs.
switches	Internal - specifies from within CONFIG.SYS special DOS options.

Switches:
/f   skips the 2-second delay after displaying the 'Starting MS-DOS ...' message during start-up.
/k   forces an enhanced keyboard to behave like a conventional keyboard.
/n   prevents you from using the **F5** or **F8** key to bypass start-up commands.
/w   specifies that the wina20.386 file has been moved to a directory other than the root directory.

sys   External - transfers the DOS system files from the logged drive to the disc in the specified drive. It also allows the specification of source drive and path commands to transfer system files across a network.

time   Internal - displays and sets the system time. It also supports a 12- or 24-hour format.

tree   External - displays the directory structure in graphical form.

Switches:
/a   specifies that tree is to use text characters instead of graphic characters.
/f   displays the names of the files in each directory.

type   Internal - displays the contents of a file on the console.

undelete

External - restores files which were previously deleted with the DEL command.

Switches:

/all	recovers all deleted files without prompting.
/dos	recovers only those files that are internally listed as deleted by DOS, prompting for confirmation.
/ds	recovers only those files listed in the SENTRY directory, prompting for confirmation on each file.
/dt	recovers only the files listed in the deletion-tracking file.
/list	lists deleted files that are available to be recovered.
/load	loads the memory-resident portion of the UNDELETE program.
/unload	removes the memory-resident portion of the UNDELETE program.
/purge	deletes the contents of the SENTRY directory.
/s	enables the Delete Sentry level of protection and loads the memory-resident portion of the UNDELETE program.
/status	displays the type of delete protection in effect for each drive.
/t	enables the Delete Tracker level of protection and loads the memory-resident portion of the UNDELETE program.

unformat	External - restores a disc erased by the FORMAT command or re-structured by the recover command.

Switches:

/l   when used with the /partn switch, lists every file and subdirectory found by UNFORMAT.

/p   sends output messages to the printer connected to LPT1.

/test   shows how unformat will recreate the information of the disc.

ver	Internal - displays the MS/PC-DOS version number.
verify	Internal - allows the verify switch to be turned ON or OFF.

Example: verify OFF

vol	Internal - displays the disc volume label, if it exists.
vsafe	External - monitors for viruses.
xcopy [filespec]	External - copies files and directories, including lower level sub-directories, if they exist, to the destination drive and directory.

Switches:

/a copies source files that have their archive bit set.

/d: copies source files which were modified on or after a specified date.

/e copies sub-directories even if they are empty - use this switch in conjunction with /s.

/m copies archived files only, but also turns off the archive bit in the source file.

/p prompts the user with '(Y/N?)'

/s copies directories and their sub-directories unless they are empty.

/v causes verification of each file as it is written.

/w displays a message before starting to copy.

9. GLOSSARY OF TERMS

Application — Software (program) designed to carry out certain activity, such as word processing.

ASCII — It is a binary code representation of a character set. The name stands for 'American Standard Code for Information Interchange'.

AUTOEXEC.BAT — A batch file containing commands which are automatically executed on booting up the system.

BACKUP — To make a back-up copy of a file or a disc for safekeeping.

Base memory — The first 1 Mbyte of random access memory.

BASIC — A high level programming language. The name stands for 'Beginner's All-purpose Symbolic Instruction Code'.

Batch file — An ASCII formatted file that contains MS-DOS commands which can be executed by the computer.

Baud — The unit of measurement used to describe data transmission speed. One baud is one bit per second.

BIOS — The Basic Input/Output System. It allows the core of the operating system to communicate with the hardware.

Bit	A binary digit; the smallest unit of information that can be stored, either as 1 or as 0.
Bitmap	A technique for managing the image displayed on a computer screen.
Boot	To start up the computer and load the DOS operating system.
Booting up	The process of starting up the computer.
Branching	Transferring execution of commands to another part of a batch file.
Buffer	RAM memory allocated to store data being read from disc.
Byte	A grouping of binary digits (0 or 1) which represent information.
Cache	An area of memory reserved for data, which speeds up access to a disc.
Card	A removable printed-circuit board that is plugged into an expansion slot.
CGA	Colour Graphics Adaptor; 2 modes and 4 colours - almost obsolete.
Cluster	A unit of one or more sectors. It is the minimum amount of space that can be allocated to a file on disc.
Click	To quickly press and release a mouse button.
Clipboard	An area of memory, also called a buffer, where text, graphics,

and commands can be stored to await further action.

Code page   A table in DOS that defines which extended ASCII character set is used in a document.

Cold boot   The process of starting your PC by turning on the power switch.

Command   An instruction given to a computer to carry out a particular action.

COMMAND.COM   The Operating System's Command Processor which analyses what is typed at the keyboard and causes execution of appropriate commands.

Command line   The line on the computer's screen into which you enter DOS commands.

Command Prompt   The prompt (C>) which appears on the computer's screen to let you know that MS-DOS is ready to receive a command.

CONFIG.SYS   A special file that allows the system to be configured closer to requirement.

Conventional Memory   The first 640KB of base memory, used by DOS programs.

Coprocessor   A processor for doing specialist tasks, such as a maths coprocessor. It reduces the load on the CPU.

CPU   The Central Processing Unit; the main chip that executes all instructions entered into a computer.

Current directory	The directory that is searched first for a requested file.
Cursor	The blinking line indicating where the next input can be entered.
Default	The command, device or option automatically chosen by the system.
Device driver	A special file that must be loaded into memory for DOS to be able to address a specific procedure or hardware device. These are normally installed from the CONFIG.SYS file at system start-up.
Device name	A logical name used by DOS to identify a device, such as LPT1 or COM1 for the parallel or serial printer.
Dialogue box	A box that MS-DOS displays on the screen when DOSSHELL is in operation, to ask the user for more information.
Directory	An area on disc where information relating to a group of files is kept.
Directory identifier	Displays the active disc drive and directory on the File System screen of DOSSHELL.
Directory tree	A pictorial representation of your disc's structure.
Disc	A device on which you can store programs and data.

Disc file	A collection of program code, or data, that is stored under a given name on a disc.
DOS	The Disc Operating System. A collection of small specialised programs that allow interaction between user and computer.
DOS Extender	Software that allows DOS programs to run in extended memory.
DOS prompt	The prompt displayed on the screen, such as A> or C>, indicating that DOS is ready to accept commands when not working with DOSSHELL.
DOSSHELL	The name of the front-end graphical interface provided by MS-DOS 5.
Double-click	To quickly press and release a mouse button twice.
DPI	Dots Per Inch - a resolution standard for laser printers.
DR-DOS	Digital Research's (now owned by Novell) implementation of the Disc Operating System for compatible PCs.
Drag	To press and hold down the left mouse button while moving the mouse.
Drive name	The letter followed by a colon which identifies a floppy or hard disc drive.
Driver	A set of commands used to run a peripheral device (see device driver).

Edit	The MS-DOS screen editor which is used to create and modify ASCII formatted files, such as batch files, and the CONFIG.SYS file.
EGA	Enhanced Graphics Adaptor; it has 6 modes and 16 colours.
EISA	Extended Industry Standard Architecture, for construction of PCs with the Intel 32 bit microprocessor.
EMM	Expanded Memory Manager.
Emulate	To make one process act like another with the use of special hardware or software.
Enter key	The key that must be pressed after entering data.
EMS	The Expanded Memory Specification developed by Lotus, Intel and Microsoft to enable programs to use Expanded memory and provided in DOS 5 & 6 by EMM386.EXE.
Expanded memory	This is memory outside the conventional RAM (first 640K) that DOS uses. It can be used by software to store data and run applications.
Extended memory	This is memory above the 1-Mbyte memory address which DOS can use for certain operations.
External command	A command DOS executes by first loading it from an external disc file.

FAT	The File Allocation Table. An area on disc where information is kept on which part of the disc the file is to be found.
File	The name given to an area on disc containing a program or data.
File extension	The optional three-letter suffix following the period in a filename.
File list	A list of filenames contained in the active directory.
Filename	The name given to a file. It must not exceed 8 characters in length and can have an extension of up to 3 characters.
Filespec	File specification made up of drive, path, filename and a three letter extension.
Fixed disc	The hard disc of a computer.
Floppy disc	A removable disc on which information can be stored magnetically. There are two types of floppy discs; a 5¼" flexible disc and a 3½" stiff disc.
Formatting	The process of preparing a disc so that it can store information. During formatting, sectors, tracks, a directory, and the FAT are created on the disc.
Function key	One of the series of 10 or 12 keys marked with the letter F and a numeral, used for specific operations.
Gigabyte	1,024 megabytes.

Graphics card	A device that controls the display on the monitor and other allied functions.
GUI	A Graphical User Interface, such as that of DOSSHELL which uses visual displays to eliminate the need for typing commands.
Hardcopy	Output on paper.
Hard disc	A device built into the computer for holding programs and data. It is sometimes referred to as the fixed disc.
Hardware	The equipment that makes up a computer system, excluding the programs or software.
Help	A feature that gives you instructions and additional information on using DOS (DOS applications normally include their own help system).
Hidden files	Files that do not normally appear in a directory listing, such as the IO.SYS and MSDOS.SYS files.
Highlight	The change to a reverse-video appearance when a menu item or area of text is selected.
HIMEM.SYS	The system file that allows the use of extended memory by DOS programs.
HMA	High Memory Area; the first 64 Kbytes of memory beyond the end of the base memory, which DOS software can access.

128

Icon	A small graphic image that represents a function. Clicking on an icon produces an action.
Internal command	One of a set of many commands available to you at any time as they are loaded into memory every time you start your PC.
Interface	A device that allows you to connect a computer to its peripherals.
ISA	Industry Standard Architecture; a standard for internal connections in PCs.
Key combination	When two or more keys are pressed simultaneously, such as Ctrl+Alt+Del.
Kilobyte	(Kbyte); 1024 bytes of information or storage space.
LABEL	The MS-DOS command which allows you to give a name to your disc.
LAN	Local Area Network; PCs, workstations or minis sharing files and peripherals within the same site.
LCD	Liquid Crystal Display.
Macro	A suite of programming commands invoked by one keystroke.
MCA	Micro Channel Architecture; IBM's standard for construction of PCs introduced in the 1990s.
Megabyte	(Mbyte); 1024 kilobytes of information or storage space.

Megahertz	(MHz); Speed of processor in million of cycles per second.
Memory	Part of computer consisting of storage elements organised into addressable locations that can hold data and instructions.
Menu	A list of available options as appears in the DOSSHELL.
Menu bar	The horizontal bar that lists the names of menus.
Microprocessor	The calculating chip within a computer.
Minicomputer	A small mainframe computer to which terminals can be attached.
MIPS	Million Instructions Per Second; measures speed of a system.
Monitor	The display device connected to your PC.
Mouse	A device used to manipulate a pointer around your display and activate a certain process by pressing a button.
MS-DOS	Microsoft's implementation of the Disc Operating System for compatible PCs.
Network server	Central computer which stores files for several linked computers.
Operating System	A group of programs that translates your commands to the computer.
OS/2	An alternative operating system to DOS for powerful PCs, introduced in 1988.

Parallel interface	A device that allows transfer of blocks of data in bytes.
Parameter	Additional information appended to an MS-DOS command to indicate how the command should be executed.
PATH	The drive and directories that DOS should look in for files.
PC	Personal Computer.
PC-DOS	IBM's implementation of DOS for IBM PCs.
PCX	A standard file format used for bitmapped graphics.
Peripheral	Any device attached to a PC.
Pixel	A picture element on screen; the smallest element that can be indepenently assigned colour and intensity.
Port	An input/output address through which your PC interacts with external devices.
Print queue	The list of print jobs waiting to be sent to a printer.
Program	A set of instructions which cause the computer to perform certain tasks.
Prompt	The System prompt displayed on screen, such as A> or C>, indicating that DOS is ready to accept commands.
Protected mode	The operating mode of 286 (and higher) processors, not normally used by DOS. It allows more than 1 Mbyte of memory to be addressed.

Protocol	It defines the way in which data is transferred between different hardware.
Processor	The electronic device which performs calculations.
PS/2	The range of PCs first introduced by IBM in late 1980s.
RAM	Random Access Memory. The micro's volatile memory. Data held in it is lost when power is switched off.
Real mode	The normal operating mode of PCs, in which only the first 1 Mbyte of memory can be addressed.
Return key	The same as the Enter key.
ROM	Read Only Memory. The micro's non-volatile memory. Data are written into this memory at manufacture and are not affected by power loss.
Root directory	The main disc directory under which a number of subdirectories can be created.
Scroll bar	The bar that appears at the right side of the File List and Directory sections of the File System screen of DOSSHELL.
Sector	Disc space, normally 512 bytes long.
Serial interface	An interface that transfers data as individual bits; each operation has to be completed before the next starts.

SHELL	A front end to DOS or an alternative Command Processor.
Software	The programs and instructions that control your PC's functionality.
Spooler	Software which handles transfer of information to a store where it will be used by a peripheral device.
SVGA	Super Video Graphics Array; it has all the VGA modes but with 256 colours.
System	Short for computer system, implying a specific collection of hardware and software.
System disc	A disc containing DOS' three main files and other Utilities.
System prompt	The prompt displayed on the screen, such as A> or C> indicating that DOS is ready to accept commands when not working with DOSSHELL.
Text file	A file saved in ASCII format. It contains text characters, but no formatting codes.
Title bar	A horizontal bar across the top of each screen in DOSSHELL that contains the name of the screen.
Toggle	A term used to describe something that turns on and off with the same switch.
TSR	Terminate and Stay Resident programs, that is, memory resident programs.

UMB	A block of upper memory made available by a 386 memory manager into which memory resident software can be loaded.
Upper memory	The 384 Kbytes of memory between the top of conventional memory and the end of the base memory.
VGA	Video Graphics Array; has all modes of EGA, but with 16 colours.
Volume label	An identifying label written to a disc when a disc is first formatted.
Warm boot	The process of starting your PC with the use of the Ctrl+Alt+Del key combination.
Wildcard character	A character that can be included in a filename to indicate any character (?) or group of characters (*) that might match that position in other filenames.
Windows	A program developed by Microsoft in which applications can appear in graphical form.
XMS	The Extended Memory Specification developed by Microsoft to allow DOS programs to use extended memory. This is provided in DOS 5 & 6 by HIMEM.SYS.

APPENDIX A - THE DOS SHELL

The DOS Shell is not distributed with MS-DOS 6.2, but is with versions 4.0 to 6.0. If you have the program and type DOSSHELL at the C> prompt, then you will be able to see the directory tree which is displayed on the top-left part of the DOS Shell screen with a listing of the files of the logged directory (in this case the root directory) appearing on the top-right of the screen, as shown below.

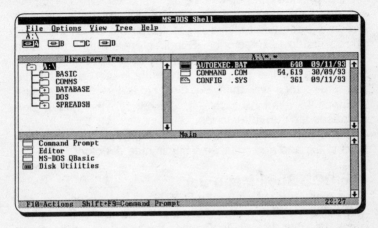

You can navigate around the DOS Shell screen, either by using the keyboard or by using a mouse.

To select an item with the keyboard, use the <Tab> key to move the cursor between screen areas, then use the vertical arrow keys to highlight the required item within the selected area and press <Enter>.

To select an item with the mouse, simply point to the required item and click the left mouse button. It is assumed, of course, that the required mouse driver is loaded according to the instructions that accompany the device. This requires you to include the command **MOUSE** within your AUTOEXEC.BAT file (more about this later).

If you have an EGA or VGA screen, the mouse pointer appears as an inclined arrow, indicating that DOS Shell is in 'Graphics' mode, otherwise for a CGA screen it appears as a small square, indicating that DOS Shell is in 'Text' mode. You can change modes by using the <Alt+O> command (press the <Alt> key and while holding it down, press the letter <O>) to reveal the pull-down **Options** menu and select the **Display** option, either by pointing with the mouse and clicking the left mouse button, or by using the down arrow key to highlight it and pressing <Enter>. A selection box appears in the middle of the screen from which you can select the required mode.

As seen earlier, the same directory tree as the one shown on the previous page, can be obtained by the use of the external DOS command 'tree' (DOS 4 or higher). The two directory trees differ slightly in so far as the DOS Shell only shows first-level directories. Subdirectories with a plus sign (+) against their name in the directory tree, can be expanded by clicking on the plus sign. The subdirectories under the given directory will then be displayed and the plus sign changes to a minus sign (−). Clicking on the minus sign collapses the sub- directories.

If you don't have a mouse, use the grey <+> or grey <−> keys to expand and collapse a highlighted directory.

The DOS Shell Menu Bar

Each menu bar option on the DOS Shell has associated with it a pull-down sub-menu. To activate the menu bar, either press the <Alt> key, which causes the first item on the menu bar (in this case **File**) to be highlighted, then use the right and left arrow keys to highlight any of the items of the menu bar, or use the mouse to point to an item. Pressing either <Enter> or the left mouse button, reveals the pull-down sub-menu.

The pull-down sub-menus can also be activated directly by pressing the <Alt> key followed by the first letter of the required menu option. Thus pressing <Alt+O>, causes the **Options** sub-menu to be displayed. Use the up and down arrow keys to move the highlighted bar up and down within a sub-menu, or the right and left arrow keys to move along the options of the menu bar. Pressing the <Enter> key selects the highlighted option, while pressing the <Esc> key closes the menu system.

The Menu Bar Options:

Each item of the menu bar offers several options which are described on the following pages. However, dimmed or not visible command names indicate that these commands are unavailable at this time; you might need to select an item before you can use such commands. The biggest difference is observed with the **Files** sub-menu and it depends on whether you are working with files or programs (you have more options available to you with files).

You can display the information given below by selecting the DOS Shell **Help, Commands** option which causes a File List and a Program List to appear on your screen. Choosing an item from these lists (by highlighting it and pressing <Enter>, or pointing at it and clicking the left mouse button) produces the information on the specific item. This same information is listed below which should make reference to it easier to access.

The File Menu with Files

When DOS Shell is first entered, or if you select an item from the File-list area, such as the AUTOEXEC.BAT file, and then choose **File**, the following menu is displayed:

Open: Starts a selected program and an associated file, if there is one.

Run: Displays a dialogue box in which you type the name of the program file that starts the program.

Print: Prints the selected text file(s). The Print command only works if you have run PRINT.COM at the command prompt.

Associate: Associates all files having the same extension with a program, or a selected file with a program so that starting the program automatically loads the specified file.

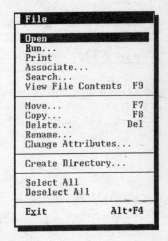

```
File

Open
Run...
Print
Associate...
Search...
View File Contents    F9

Move...                F7
Copy...                F8
Delete...              Del
Rename...
Change Attributes...

Create Directory...

Select All
Deselect All

Exit              Alt+F4
```

Search: Finds files on all or part of the currently selected disc drive.

View File Contents: Displays the contents of the selected text file or binary file.

Move: Moves the selected file(s) from one directory to a directory you specify.

Copy: Copies one or more files in one directory to a directory you specify.

Delete: Deletes selected files or directories.

Rename: Renames a selected file or directory to the name you specify.

Change Attributes: Displays the attributes assigned to a file, such as Hidden, System, Archive, and Read-Only. Use this command to change these attributes.

Create Directory: Creates a new directory on the current drive. If a directory is selected, it creates a subdirectory within that directory.

Select All: Selects all files in the currently selected directory.

Deselect All: Cancels all selections except one in the currently selected directory.

Exit: Quits DOS Shell and returns to the system prompt.

The File Menu with Programs

If you select an item from the Program-list area of the Main group of programs, such as the **Editor**, and then choose **File,** the following menu is displayed:

New: Adds a new group or program item to the currently selected group.

Open: Starts a program and an associated file (if any), or displays the contents of a group.

138

Copy: Copies a program item to the group you specify. After choosing the command, open the group you want to copy to, and then press **F2**.

Delete: Deletes the selected group, or program item, from a group. Before deleting a group, you must delete all of its program items.

Properties: Specifies for a program item, the title, the command that starts the program, the start-up directory for the program to use, an application shortcut key, Help text, a password, and other properties.

Reorder: Moves the selected program item or group from its current location to the location you specify.

Run: Displays a dialogue box in which you type the name of the program file that starts the program.

Exit: Quits DOS Shell and returns to the system prompt.

Options Menu

Selecting **Options** when working with either files or programs, displays the following pull-down menu:

Confirmation: Specifies if DOS Shell should prompt you for confirmation before deleting files or replacing files with duplicate names.

File Display Options: Lists files in sequence by name, extension, date, size, or order on disc. Also controls the display of Hidden or System files.

Select Across Directories: Controls whether or not you can select files in more than one directory. A mark next to the command indicates that it is active.

Show Information: Displays information on the selected file(s), directory and disc.

Enable Task Swapper: Turns on or off task swapping and displays the Active Task List to the right of the

Program List. With this on, you can have more than one program open at a time and switch between them. A mark next to the command indicates that it is on.

Display: Changes screen mode and the resolution used to display DOS Shell.

Colors: Changes the colour scheme used for DOS Shell.

View Menu

Selecting **View** when working with either files or programs, displays a pull-down menu. With files, there is an additional 'Refresh' command, as shown below:

Single File List: Displays a single directory tree and file list for the current drive.

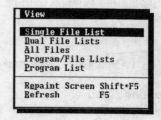

Dual File List: Displays two directory trees and file lists for the selected drive(s) in the file list.

All Files: Lists every file on the current drive, as well as information about the drive, its directories, and its files.

Program/File Lists: Causes the display of a list of directories and files and a list of groups and programs.

Program List: Displays a list of groups and program items in the current group.

Repaint Screen: Redraws the screen, but does not update the list of files. For the latter to happen, use the 'Refresh' command.

Refresh: Rereads the disc and updates the list to show changes caused by such actions as deleting or restoring files.

Tree Menu

This menu option is only available when you are working with files. Selecting **Tree** displays the following pull-down menu.

Expand One Level: Displays the next level of sub-directories for the selected directory in the Directory tree.

Expand Branch: Displays all levels of subdirectories in the selected directory in the Directory Tree.

Expand All: Displays all subdirectories in the Directory Tree.

Collapse Branch: Hides all currently displayed sub-directories in the selected directory in the Directory Tree.

Help Menu

Selecting **Help** when working with either files or programs, displays the following pull-down menu:

Index: Displays the DOS Shell Help Index.

Keyboard: Displays a list of shortcut keys you can use with DOS Shell.

Shell Basics: Displays a list of topics for basic skills you need to work with DOS Shell.

Commands: Displays a list of all DOS Shell commands, grouped by menu.

Procedures: Displays a list of topics you can look at for help on DOS Shell tasks.

Using Help: Displays a list of topics which explain how to use DOS Shell Help.

File Selection in DOS Shell:

To select a single file or multiple files while in DOS Shell, use either the mouse or the keyboard. The procedure is as follows:

- To select a single file: With the mouse, click the name of the file, while with the keyboard use the arrow keys to highlight it.

- To select two or more contiguous files: With the mouse, click the first filename you want to select, then press down the <Shift> key while you click the last filename of the block. With the keyboard, use the arrow keys to highlight the first filename in the list, then press down the <Shift> key and while holding it down use the arrow keys to highlight the block of filenames.

- To select two or more non-contiguous files: With the mouse, press and hold down the <Ctrl> key while you click at the required filenames, while with the keyboard select the first filename then press <Shift+**F8**> and move to the next filename, press the <Spacebar> to select the highlighted filename, go the next filename and press <Spacebar>, and so on, until you have finished when you press <Shift+**F8**>.

The DOS Shell, gives a graphical way of easily manipulating your files and directories, without having to learn all the command names. There is a down side though; while it is active it uses valuable RAM memory. You may not be able to use it and run very large application programs at the same time.

APPENDIX B - THE EDLIN LINE EDITOR

MS-DOS provides pre-DOS 5 users with a simple line editor, called **Edlin**, and you should become familiar with its use. In general, **Edlin** allows the creation and editing of ASCII files. These are text files which when sent to the screen or printer are interpreted as text, unlike the .COM or .EXE files which are binary.

Edlin can also be used to create the source code of various programming languages, such as Fortran and C. In such cases, remember to give the file the appropriate extension, which for the two languages mentioned, are **.for** and **.c**, respectively. However, if you intend to write large programs which might require extensive editing, you might be better off using a full screen editor or your word processor, provided it can save files in ASCII format.

To invoke **Edlin**, the MS-DOS System disc or a disc that contains it must be in one drive, and the file you want to create or edit must be specified. Thus, typing the command

```
C:\>edlin test.txt
```

expects to find both **Edlin** and the fictitious file **test.txt** on the disc in the logged drive (in this case C:), while typing

```
C:\>edlin A:test.txt
```

expects to find **Edlin** on the disc in the logged drive and the file **test.txt** on the disc in the A: drive.

If the file does not exist on the specified disc, then **Edlin** responds with

```
New File
*_
```

and waits for further commands, while if the file already exists, then **Edlin** loads the file into RAM and responds with

```
End of input file
*_
```

Note the '*' prompt which is characteristic of **Edlin**.

Let us now create a text file, called TEST.TXT, which we will use to demonstrate the power of **Edlin**. To start, type at the MS-DOS prompt

```
C:\>edlin test.txt
```

which should cause **Edlin** to respond with

```
New File
*_
```

if that file does not exist on your disc. If it does exist and you do not want to spoil its contents, then type **q** (for quit) and press the <Enter> key.

The Insert Command on a New File

To insert lines of text, use the command **i** (for insert) at the prompt. In the case of a new file, as no lines of text exist in the file, type 1i and then type in the short text given below.

```
*1i
    1:*first line of text
    2:*second line of text
    3:*^C
*_
```

After typing 1i at the prompt, **Edlin** responds by giving a new line number (in this case 1:) with an asterisk after it to indicate that this is the current line. At this point we type 'first line of text'. On pressing the <Enter> key, **Edlin** gives us an additional line number, now 2:*, into which we type 'second line of text'. Again, on pressing <Enter>, we are offered a further line number, and so on. To end the insertion mode, press <Ctrl+C>. The character **^C** is the two-key depression <Ctrl+C> (hold the key marked <Ctrl> down and press the <C> key).

144

The List Command

To see what text is in the file, type **1** (for list) at the prompt, as follows:

```
*1
   1: first line of text
   2:*second line of text
*_
```

The line numbers are inserted by **Edlin** so that you can refer to the line you want to edit. The '*' in line 2 indicates that this line was the last to be edited or inserted when **Edlin** was used last. Note that now there is only one current line. Should the file you are listing be very long, listing in this manner causes the current line to appear in the middle of the listing.

To list specific lines, use the **1** command with line numbers. For example,

```
*5,151
```

will list lines from 5 to 15 inclusive. Note the syntax of the command which is: 'From line number to line number Command'. There must be no comma between the second line number and the command letter.

The Edit Mode

To change the current line, type the new line number and press <Enter>. This puts you in edit mode and will cause the line whose number you typed to be displayed. Pressing <Enter> again, confirms that you are happy with the contents of that line, otherwise you can either press the right cursor key to reveal each letter of that line, or re-type the entire line, making any necessary changes. In our case, we want to change line 2 to

```
second line of text, edited
```

so enter the edit mode and change the line appropriately. This is best done by using the right arrow cursor key to reveal the whole of the existing line and then typing the extra information at the end of it. The **Ins** and **Del** keys can also be used to edit the text.

145

The Insert Command on an Existing File

To insert lines of text, use the command **i** (for insert) at the prompt. However, be warned. Using **i** by its own will insert the new line before the current line (the one with the * after the line number). To insert lines at any other point, give the line number before the command.

In our case, we would like to insert two additional lines after the existing two. To do this, type

```
*3i
   3:*third line of text
   4:*fourth line of text
   5:*^C
*_
```

Again, insertion mode is terminated in line 5: by pressing **Ctrl+C**. If we now list the contents of the file, we get:

```
*1
   1: first line of text
   2: second line of text, edited
   3: third line of text
   4:*fourth line of text
*_
```

The last line to be inserted becomes the current line.

The Delete Command

To delete unwanted lines of text, use the **d** command (for delete) at the prompt. However, if you use the **d** command without any number associated with it, you will delete the current line (the one with the asterisk). Therefore, if you want to delete line 13, say, type

```
*13d
```

or if you want to delete a group of lines, type

```
*13,15d
```

which is translated as 'lines 13 to 15 to be deleted'.

The Move & Copy Commands

To move or copy text, use the **m** or **c** commands (for move or copy). These commands must be preceded by three numbers, as follows:

```
*13,15,8m
```

which is interpreted as 'lines 13 to 15 to be moved to a position before line 8'.

Similarly, the **c** command will copy a block and insert it before the given line. To move or copy a single line, the first two numbers in the command will have to be the same. After moving or copying lines, always use the list command to force re-numbering of the file's contents.

The Search Command

To search for the occurrence of a word or a specified number of characters in a file you have created using **Edlin**, use the search command. Just as in the list and delete commands, a line range is first specified, followed by the **s** (for search) command. Thus, typing

```
*1,4s edited
```

evokes the response

```
   2: second line of text, edited
*_
```

which displays the line containing the word 'edited'.

Note that the space between the command **s** and the word 'edited' becomes part of the search string. Had we been searching for the characters 'con' within the word 'second', we would have had to omit the space between the command s and the string 'con'.

The search command finds only the first occurrence of the specified string. To continue the search for further occurrences of the same string, simply type **s** again.

Thus, typing

```
*1,4sir
   1: first line of text
*s
   3: third line of text
*_
```

causes **Edlin** to first find the string 'ir' in the word 'first' of line 1:, then by typing **s** again, it forces **Edlin** to find the same string 'ir' in the word 'third' of line 3:.

The Search & Replace Command

This command is similar to the search command, except that it requires a replacement string. Thus, typing

```
*1,4r edited^Z re-edited
```

will cause all occurrences of the word 'edited' to be replaced by the word 're-edited' in all the specified lines of text. Here, of course, it only occurs once in line 2: of the text. The character **^Z** is the two-key depression <Ctrl+Z> (hold the key marked <Ctrl> down and press the <Z> key), which acts as a delimiter between the two strings. Again note that the space in front of both words becomes part of both the searching and the replacing strings.

The Transfer Command

This command transfers the contents of a file into the file currently being edited. The format of the command is:

[n] T filespec

where

n   specifies the line number where the new data is to be inserted. The data is inserted before the specified line. If the line number is omitted, then the current line is used.

filespec   specifies the file that you want to insert the contents of into the current file in memory.

148

Exiting Edlin

To end the current session and exit **Edlin** at any point, type

    *e

which saves a new file under the chosen filename.

However, if the filename already existed on disc prior to using **Edlin**, ending **Edlin** has the following effect:

> First the name of the old file on the disc is given the extension .BAK, then the new file you have created by editing the old one is saved with the original extension. In this way you can make mistakes without disastrous effects since the system makes a back-up file of the original. If need be, you could delete the .TXT file and then rename the back-up file (.BAK) to its original name and extension.

Note that **Edlin** is disciplined not to allow editing of back-up files so, should you want to start using **Edlin** to edit the contents of a .BAK file, you must first rename it, by giving it a different extension, before proceeding.

If, on the other hand, you realised that too many mistakes were made during editing, you could use the **q** command to quit, as follows:

    *q

instead of using the **e** command as discussed above. Doing this causes **Edlin** to ask you whether you want to abort. Typing **y** (for yes), leaves the name and contents of the original file on disc unaltered.

INDEX

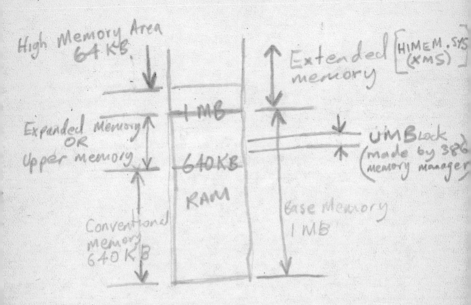

High Memory Area
64 KB.

Extended memory $\begin{bmatrix} \text{HIMEM.SYS} \\ (\text{XMS}) \end{bmatrix}$

1 MB

Expanded Memory
OR
Upper memory

UMBlock
(made by 386
memory manager)

640 KB
RAM

Conventional
memory
640 KB

Base Memory
1 MB

NOTES

NOTES

NOTES

COMPANION DISC TO THIS BOOK

This book contains many pages of file/program listings. There is no reason why you should spend hours typing them into your computer, unless you wish to do so, or need the practice.

The COMPANION DISC for this book comes with all the example listings. It is available in both 3.5-inch and 5.25-inch formats.

COMPANION DISCS for all books written by the same author(s) and published by BERNARD BABANI (publishing) LTD, are also available and are listed at the front of this book. Make sure you fill in your name and address and specify the book number, title and the disc size in your order.

ORDERING INSTRUCTIONS

To obtain your copy of the companion disc, fill-in the order form below, enclose a cheque (payable to **P.R.M. Oliver**) or a postal order, and send it to the address given below.

Book No.	Book Name	Unit Price	Total Price
BP		£3.50	
BP		£3.50	
BP		£3.50	
Name .... Address		Sub-total	£.............
		P & P (@ 45p/disc)	£.............
Disc Format 3.5-inch....... 5.25-inch......		Total Due	£.............
Send to: P.R.M. Oliver, CSM, Pool, Redruth, Cornwall, TR15 3SE			